VOLUME 1

INDIAN MUSIC

VOLUME 1

INDIAN MUSIC

Swami Rama

The Himalayan International Institute
of Yoga Science and Philosophy
of the U.S.A.
Honesdale, Pennsylvania

*Himalayan International Institute
of Yoga Science and Philosophy of the U.S.A.
RR 1, Box 400
Honesdale, Pennsylvania 18431*

Second Printing 1996

Library of Congress Cataloging-in-Publication Data

Rama, Swami, 1925-
    Indian music.

    1. Singing—Instruction and study. 2. Music, Hindustani—Instruction and study. 3.
Music—Instruction and study—India. I. Title.
MT850.R34 1989   784.9'32   88-35815
ISBN 0-89389-113-4 (v.1)

CONTENTS

ACKNOWLEDGMENTS

I wish to acknowledge the efforts of the Institute staff in the preparation of this book. Rolf Sovik and many others read the manuscript. Pandit Rajmani Tigunait translated the original manuscript from Hindi to English. Devika Nichols assisted in preparing the manuscript and the glossary. Cover design is by Vicki Roser, based on a photograph from Carol Kingsbury. Kamal Hafford typeset the final manuscript.

INTRODUCTION

THE BENEFITS OF SINGING

Some ten years ago, while visiting Boulder, Colorado, I suffered a serious injury to my head. I was diagnosed by experts in the United States as suffering from an undefinable internal hemorrhage, for which there was neither medicine nor curative treatment. A complication of the injury was that I lost a good part of my ability to speak. No one could understand my words.

Those whose voice has been damaged or who have difficulty speaking know that one prescription for this problem is speech therapy. The methods used in speech therapy train and strengthen one's voice and make it melodious. In ancient India, the science of speech therapy was part of the discipline of music, and anyone needing voice training might well have been sent to a vocal teacher. Speech therapy as a separate science did not really exist. It was only more recently in the West that the science of speech therapy was thoroughly researched and expanded into a clinical discipline. Now, there are numerous books on the subject, and this science has become a very systematic collection of methods for culturing and training the human voice.

Following my injury, I followed a very rigorous schedule, which included both changes in my diet and the practice of special breathing exercises. These exercises, particularly the *pranayama* practices, helped me to recover from the constant bleeding problem. But my voice still remained distorted and difficult to understand. It was then that I visited many speech therapy clinics in America and Europe.

During that time, I found that certain vocal exercises taken from the musical tradition of India were very therapeutic for me. I practiced singing the vowels of the alphabet, beginning my practice at four o'clock in the morning. I used various

INDIAN MUSIC

Indian melodies, such as the well-known *Bhairav, Jogiya,* and *Bhairavi* raags. I sang no words to the music but used only vowel sounds to produce the notes. It took me six months to recover the ability to speak and lecture again, but during that time I was certainly impressed by the versatility and power of these ancient Indian musical techniques.

Actually, I had first learned the techniques of Indian vocal music in my youth, during the time in which I lived in the cave monasteries of the Himalayas. There, I used to practice six to seven hours a day to learn the various vocal exercises that make up the Indian tradition of voice culture. One day, the monks with whom I lived began to question me. They were surprised and shocked that I was singing "love songs" (in my language called "thumri") in the monastery. They reminded me that I was a renunciate and that such songs should not be sung by someone like me. After much discussion, I was instructed by my master to completely stop my singing, and to begin meditating and contemplating instead. He asked me not to sing or practice Indian classical music again until at least 1985.

I followed my master's orders and put the desire for classical music in the bed of my unconscious mind. I followed his instructions literally. Thus, it was only recently, when I visited India, that I looked into my old diaries and again began following the method of musical voice culture. This method had been given to me by Chand Khansahab. I also met Pandit Jonwari Kar of Poona, a disciple of Shri Aman Ali Khan, a great singer and composer of his time. I started practicing the subtle methods of Indian vocalization taught by Aman Ali Khan, which are called *Khanda Gayaki.* His method teaches how to use a particular note in various ways without distorting it. His techniques helped me so much that I can sing once again the melodies that I used to sing in my youth.

Indian classical music is as ancient as the human race itself. Among the *Vedas,* the most ancient scriptures in the library of man, the *Sama Veda* is devoted to the art of music. How fortunate is he or she who loves to sing or play an instrument! Indian classical music is deep, profound, and melodious. It draws upon the rhythms of nature that resonate in the human heart. Everyone can respond to it.

In fact, a life without art is vacant. Singing, playing instruments, dancing, painting, and composing poetry are all various methods of expressing human emotions in a creative way. If these emotions are not expressed and directed in pleasant ways, they can cause psychosomatic diseases. Recently, scientists have begun to realize that numerous diseases actually have their origins in human thought and emotion, and are merely reflected in the body and in human behavior. Music, being the highest method of expressing emotions, can be useful as a therapy for certain problems.

Permit me to say that the many diseases of man are being researched here, there, and everywhere, but nowhere is there a research center helping people to rid themselves of the great inborn disease of human beings—loneliness. Every human being is lonely. Loneliness is actually the leading cause of death—only then followed by strokes, heart disease, and cancer—and it may even have a role in their development as well. Music, if used as either a preventive therapy or as a cure, can be a wonderful and powerful method of removing that great killer called loneliness.

Among the different forms of music, singing is the first and most powerful. Next in order of importance comes the ability to produce music by playing instruments. At our Institute we are conducting experiments by teaching people to learn to sing and to play various instruments. When I observe the effects of music on these students, it is evident that those who acquire the taste for singing or playing instruments are happier than those who do not. Surely, if music is properly taught, it can help many. Its importance is overlooked and underestimated.

Understanding Indian music may seem difficult at first to the Western listener. To the Western ear, it seems that there is something hauntingly beautiful, yet exotic and foreign about the melodies, rhythms, and timbres of Indian classical music. It is as if a lovely musical image is being whispered to the Western listener, but in a language that he or she does not quite understand. The Westerner may wonder what gives Indian music its special qualities. How is the voice taught to sing, and the ear taught to hear and understand, the language that this music uses so adeptly? These are the questions that this book is intended to answer.

The best way to learn Indian music is to begin practicing it, and the best way to practice is to actually sing. According to the *Sangita Ratnagar,* an authoritative scripture on Indian music written by Sarangadev, "the combination of vocal and instrumental performance, as well as dance, is called music." The same scripture points out that, while dance follows rhythm, the instruments follow melody, and of all instruments, the voice is the central focus in Indian music.

There are two main schools of Indian music—Hindustani music and Karnatic music. They are associated with the north and south regions of India respectively. It is the Hindustani school that is explained in this book. This school is most widely practiced both within and outside India.

In order to gain real expertise in this practice, it will be necessary to have some familiarity with the technical terms of Indian music. This book will be most useful to those students who already have some applied experience with the study of Indian music. Western musicians will be pleased to find that there are similarities in their own training and the fundamentals of Indian theory and practice. However, both the Indian methods of learning to produce music, and the theory of the music itself are unique, and offer challenges to beginning and experienced students.

Depending on your present level of experience, you will find two sections of this book helpful in getting started with your lessons. First, a Pronunciation Guide to the sounds of the Hindi/Sanskrit alphabet is located at the back of this book. It is particularly important to learn how to pronounce the vowels properly, as these sounds form the basis for vocal practice. If you are not familiar with these sounds, then review the pronunciation guide and take time to practice saying each sound aloud. While it may take some time and attention for you to learn these vowels, it is important to produce the sounds properly, so that you benefit fully from the exercises.

Secondly, the next chapter will define and explain the key and essential terms you need to understand in order to begin the study of Indian music. This section provides students with considerable detail in its explanation of the major technical terms, and it may seem somewhat challenging to those without a music background. If you patiently and thoughtfully study the terms, however, you will find it helpful. Be patient; it takes a little time and practice to learn any new language— and music is definitely a new language. You will probably not remember the definition of each term after a single reading; that doesn't matter. As you begin your vocal practice, you can refer back to the definition whenever you find it necessary.

The balance of this book is practical instruction in the art of singing Indian music. You will find that the section on vocal methods (Chapter II) will give you a good framework with which to begin. All the examples and exercises you will need are provided in Chapters IV and V. As in any learning process, it is very helpful to have a teacher who can provide a living example, and sometimes a book like this can be the inspiration to find such a teacher. However, this book itself offers a complete introduction to vocal music training, which will take students a considerable distance in their own practice.

As you begin your study do not forget the saying, "If you have the grace of God, Guru, and the scriptures, but do not have the grace of your Atma, your own higher Self, you will not attain what you want." A competent teacher is important. Then, a burning desire, sincere effort, and right guidance can make you a great musician.

CHAPTER ONE

THE LANGUAGE
OF INDIAN MUSIC

One definition of music that may be familiar to many Western readers is that music can be considered to be "organized sound." Typically, sounds have two major attributes or characteristics: *pitch* and *duration*. Pitch describes whether a sound is high or low. Duration refers to the fact that sounds occur in time—they are either long or short. Variations in the pitch and duration of sounds help to create the many possible organizations of sound called music.

The common spatial organization of sound in the West is the *octave*. An octave spans an interval of eight notes. This interval is created when the frequency of the vibration of the highest note of the octave is exactly twice that of the lowest note.

Within the octave are the seven notes (or twelve half-steps) of the scale—notes that are essentially shared by both Indian and Western music. The theoretical ways of understanding and organizing the tones of the scale differ between East and West, however. These differences in organization lead to differences in musical practice. The easiest way to learn the Indian system is to actually learn the Hindi terms and vocabulary that Indian musicians use. These terms describe the *scale,* the melodic forms that are derived from the scale, and the variety of rhythms that are used to organize these tones and melodies in time.

Nada

The word *nada* means "sound," or that which is heard by the human ear. There are two types of nada: those that are pleasing to the ear or musical, and those that are dissonant and non-musical. Nada is sound produced through the regular and constant vibration of some object in space. To vibrate, an object must have a quality of elasticity. When the equilibrium of an object is disturbed (for example, by striking it, hitting it, shaking it, or rubbing it against another object), then sound is produced. Such sound is called: *ahata nada,* or "struck sound."

In deep meditation, the yogi actually hears another type of nada. There is no sound in the external world that corresponds to this internal one. This eternal inner sound vibrates in space (*akasha*) without apparent cause. It is called *anahata nada,* or "unstruck sound." This text will focus on the external sound, or ahata nada, of music.

Ahata nada has three qualitites or characteristics that can be used to describe it:

1) Its *magnitude* (or loudness) is the degree to which it can be heard at longer or shorter distances.

2) The *frequency* (or speed) of the vibration that produces a sound gives the sound a distinctive *pitch.* A rapid vibration produces high pitch. Slow vibration produces low pitch.

3) The quality of the sound that distinguishes one person's voice from another's, or one instrument from another, even when singing or playing at the same pitch or loudness, is called *"timbre."* It is the distinctive tone of that particular voice or instrument.

Swara

A swara is a musical tone or note. When either a vocalist or instrumentalist produces a sound, it is a swara. Swaras are the audible tones of music.

A swara is a very basic sound or note. For example, when you say the letter 'a' (pronounced as the 'a' in "aloud"), the sound of your voice is cut short and is not musical. If, however, you lengthen the 'a' even a little, holding it out—you will find that you are singing, and a musical tone has been manifested. Such a tone is a swara. As we noted earlier, the swaras within the octave are organized in the form of a *scale.* The seven principle (or whole) tones of a scale are called the *saptak.* Below is a diagram showing the saptak and giving the name of each of the *shuddh swaras.* When a swara is natural or pure it is termed shuddh. When all seven swaras of a scale are natural or pure (shuddh) they form a *major scale.* The diagram below shows the seven notes of the saptak or scale. For clarity, the octave or eighth note is also shown in parentheses:

1	2	3	4	5	6	7	(8)
sa	re	ga	ma	pa	dha	ni	(sa)

The saptak (scale)

These correspond to the Western names of the pure swaras: *do, re, mi, fa, sol, la, ti,* and *do.*

In practice, of course, there are more than seven swaras that are used in forming scales, so many different scales can be formed. As in Western music, some of the seven swaras can be raised or lowered (creating sharps and flats). Indian music makes a useful distinction between swaras that can be changed in this way and swaras that cannot. Two swaras, *sa* (1) and *pa* (5), are never raised or lowered. They are never sharp or flat, and are always shuddh or pure. They are unchanging and steady, and are called *achala* (unchanging). The other swaras of the saptak are "unsteady." They are thus called *chala,* or changeable.

Among the swaras that are chala, or changeable, there are two categories. Some swaras are *komal* (soft, or flat). That is, the pure swara has been changed by being lowered in pitch. The swaras *re, ga, dha,* and *ni* can be changed in this manner. A swara can also be raised in pitch from its pure tone. Such a swara is *tivra,* or sharp. This can be done only with the swara *ma.*

The diagram above illustrates how these different swaras are organized and named. You can see that only the seven names you have already learned are used. In the notation for the raising or lowering of a swara, the following system is traditional: If the swara is komal (flat) the name is underlined. For example, re indicates lowered re, or komal re. If the swara is tivra (sharp), the name has a vertical line drawn over it. For example, *ma* indicates raised or sharp ma. Finally, when a note that was shuddh (pure) is raised or lowered, it is then called *vikrit.* Swaras are thus of two kinds: *shuddh* (the natural notes of the "major" scale), and *vikrit* (flats or sharps).

Saptak

If you are familiar with Western music, it may have occurred to you by now that the naming system for the swaras that is found in Indian music is similar to the Western system, called *solfagio.* The seven ascending swaras of the saptak do indeed parallel the ascending pitches of the Western scale.

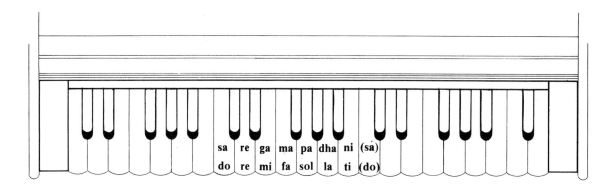

Now, if you were to sing the lowest possible note you can, and then gradually ascend using the swaras of the saptak, you would probably find that the range of your voice is more than one saptak. Indian music actually gives names to the various possible saptaks, just as Western music has named the octaves. Since instruments have a wide range of sounds, there are a number of saptaks that are outside the normal human voice range. Singers need only be familiar with three main saptaks:

Mandra saptak (lower range): the tones of this saptak are low and deep. Swaras produced from this saptak resonate in the heart region.

Madhya saptak (middle range): the swaras produced from this saptak resonate in the throat region. The sound of this range is neither too high nor too low.

Taar saptak (high range): the swaras of this saptak are high in pitch. They resonate in the region of the head.

Saptaks are indicated by dots above or below the notes. The notation below shows how the notes are written in the three main saptaks:

Mandra saptak: sa, re, ga, ma, pa, dha, ni, sa

Madhya saptak: sa, re, ga, ma, pa, dha, ni, sa

Taar saptak: sa, re, ga, ma, pa, dha, ni, sa

Varna

The movement of the singer's voice from one swara or sound to another is what eventually produces a melody. There are three main ways in which that movement can occur, and a fourth way, which combines the first three. These are called *varna*, the possible direction the notes of a melody can take, being composed of swaras that are either higher, lower, or the same as the preceding swara. The concept of the varna of a melody is easily understood: given any two swaras, the second must either be higher, lower, or the same as the first. Thus, swaras will either go up, down, or will remain the same. The direction of this movement, whether we are speaking of two swaras or eight consecutive swaras, is the varna. The three possible varnas and their combinations are:

1) Sthayi (stationary): In sthayi varna, the swaras remain the same and the note is repeated. For example: "sa, sa, sa, sa . . ."

2) Aroh (ascending): In aroh, the swaras ascend. For example:

```
                                                  sȧ
                                           ni
                                    dha
                             pa
                        ma
                   ga
              re
         sa
```

3) Avaroh (descending): In avaroh varna, the swaras descend. An example of this
    is:

```
         sȧ
              ni
                   dha
                        pa
                             ma
                                    ga
                                           re
                                                  sa
```

9

4) Sanchari varna (mixed): This fourth possible varna is a combination of the first three varnas, called sanchari. An example is given below:

<pre>
                           ga   ga   ga   ga
              re   re
    sa
</pre>

Thaat (or Mela)

By using the various raised or lowered swaras of the saptak, many possible ascending progressions or scales can be formed. Such a progression is called a *thaat* or *mela*. (Note: In pronouncing consonants followed by 'h,' remember to observe the rules found in the pronunciation guide. In this case, the 't' remains hard, not soft.) A thaat has the following characteristics:

1. In the thaat, the swaras are given only in ascending order, not in descending order.
2. A thaat itself is never sung, but rather, the melodic compositions called *raags* (see following section) that are born or derived from thaats are sung.
3. It is not necessary for a thaat to be musically pleasing to the ear.
4. The order of swaras in the saptak cannot be disturbed in constructing a thaat. The order is always: sa, re, ga, ma, pa, dha, ni, sȧ.

In the Northern Indian (Hindustani) school of music, there are ten main thaats. The first is the same as the scale that is called in the West the "major" scale. (Musicians will notice other similarities between the thaats and certain Western scales.) A complete list of the names and compositions of the ten main thaats is given below, using Indian notation and illustrations of the keyboard.

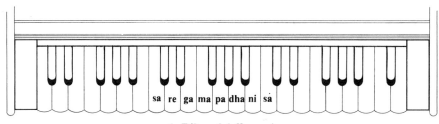

1. Bilawal (all pure)

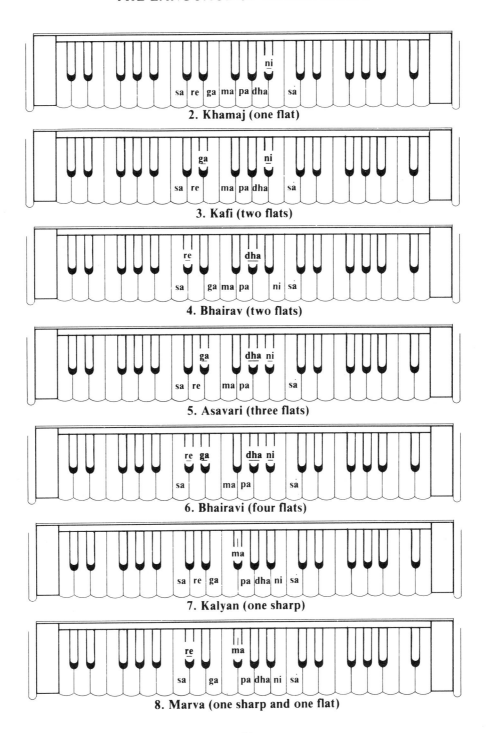

2. Khamaj (one flat)

3. Kafi (two flats)

4. Bhairav (two flats)

5. Asavari (three flats)

6. Bhairavi (four flats)

7. Kalyan (one sharp)

8. Marva (one sharp and one flat)

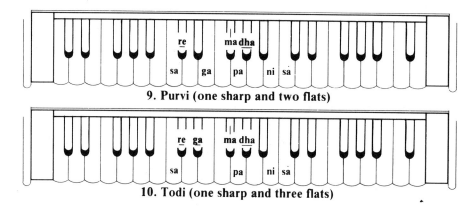

9. Purvi (one sharp and two flats)

10. Todi (one sharp and three flats)

Shruti

The *shrutis* are microtones, the smallest variation in nada that can be detected or discriminated by the trained ear. Before proceeding to the final two subjects—the melodic compositions called *raags* and the rhythmic patterns called *taals*—it is important to understand the subject of shruti in some detail. It is this subject more than any other, that has proven difficult for Western minds and for the Western ear to grasp. And yet without understanding the idea of shruti, some of the subtle nuances of classical Indian music will be missed.

There are both theoretical and practical sides to this subject of *shrutis*. The theoretical aspects will be discussed first. A shruti is first and foremost an interval or gradation in the saptak or scale. Any particular interval must somehow be related to the relationship of one tone to another fixed tone. In Indian music, the fixed tone has been given the name "sa." All the swaras are related to sa, and their position relative to sa (or their interval) is what gives them their importance. Without such a relationship, an individual note cannot really be called a swara.

The simplest example of such a relationship is the interval of the octave. One note is said to be the octave of another fixed note if it has a vibrational rate exactly twice as fast as the first note. Experience tells us that when such a relationship exists between the vibrations of two notes, then the upper note will have the harmonious sound that the ear identifies as the octave.

When the ratio of the vibration of one note to another is 3:2, the interval is recognized by the ear as the perfect fifth. When the interval is 4:3, then a perfect fourth is formed. These are relatively simple relationships of one pitch to another. However, there is no theoretical reason that one could not go on forming infinitely many intervals. This is where the practical side of the discussion of shruti enters.

In practice, there is a limit to the ability of the ear to distinguish musical intervals. The Indian system of music suggests that the ear can easily distinguish sixty-six intervals within the space of one octave. Further, the ear is drawn toward sounds which are "consonant" with one another. Such sounds are emotionally pleasing and meaningful. In music, twenty-two of these sixty-six intervals prove to be emotionally pleasing. These are mainly the simpler of the possible ratios. Thus, Indian music, though recognizing the possibility of forming an infinite number of intervals, has selected a limited number of intervals with which to build its music. These twenty-two intervals are the shrutis.

The twenty-two shrutis cannot really be sung distinctly, one after another, in a scale. They are a collection of pitches that are used in different modes. When any one of the shrutis is sounded, the note that is produced is a swara. For, as it is written in the *Sangita Darpana,* "the expressive sound, attractive and pleasing, which resounds immediately after the exact interval (the shruti) has manifested itself, is called swara." Thus, shruti refers to a relationship—the relationship formed with the fixed note *sa* and the other note. Music itself is relationship. Swara is the manifestation of that relationship in audible sound.

That which is sung is a swara; the shruti is the discimination that can be heard with the ear. When the musician's mind becomes one-pointed, and goes deep beyond the mire of the conscious and unconscious mind, he hears the voice of silence through his inner ear. When one's whole being becomes an "ear," one hears the voice of silence. The ancient seers, in their experiences of deep meditation and contemplation, heard a sound which is called the anahata nada. This nada, in manifestation, becomes a swara, but the shrutis cannot be sung. Fortunate are those few who have the profound knowledge of shrutis. It is the swaras, however, the more basic external sounds, that are sung and produced by every musician and singer.

Raag

We have seen how ten main thaats, or melas, are formed with the various swaras of the saptak. As the text, the *Abhinava Raga Manjari* notes, "the combination of swaras is called mela (thaat). This mela has the capacity to manifest a raag or raags." Now, what is a raag? Of course the easiest way to answer that question would be to listen to a raag—and many recordings are available. But we can also describe what a raag is in words that will help us to more clearly identify the important characteristics of a raag.

A raag (or *raga,* in Sanskrit) is a special composition, which draws upon swaras and varnas and is related to a particular thaat, in order to create a pleasing musical experience for listeners. The composition of a raag follows set rules. Through the raag, the musician conveys subtle feelings to an audience. The reader will find complete examples of raags for singing in Chapter Four.

Before the raags listed in Chapter Four can be sung, however, some important characteristics of raags need to be understood. While the following information is somewhat theoretical, a clear understanding of it will assist in your progress. First, there are some rules of composition for a raag.

1. A raag must use at least five of the seven swaras in the saptak.
2. There must be both aroh (ascending) and avaroh (descending) swaras in a raag.
3. A raag must be derived from one of the thaats.
4. In a raag, *ma* and *pa* cannot both be omitted.
5. A raag must contain the swara *sa.*
6. A raag must be pleasing to the ear.

The above rules are the basic criteria for composition, which will be examined in greater detail below.

The Jati of a Raag

The classification of a raag based on the number of swaras it contains, is called *jati.* There are three main jatis:

1. *Sampurn jati:* raags in which all seven swaras of the saptak are used.
2. *Shadhav jati:* raags that use only six of the seven swaras.
3. *Audav jati:* raags that use only five of the seven swaras.

A raag must both ascend (aroh) and descend (avaroh). So if a raag (and this is quite possible) were to use seven notes ascending and only six notes descending, then it would not fit into one of these three main jati categories. Thus, on the basis of the aroh and avaroh, the threefold classification of raags is further subdivided into nine:

Aroh / (Ascending /	Avaroh / Descending)	Number of Swaras	
sampurn /	sampurn	7 /	7
sampurn /	shadhav	7 /	6
sampurn /	audav	7 /	5
shadhav /	sampurn	6 /	7
shadhav /	shadhav	6 /	6
shadhav /	audav	6 /	5
audav /	sampurn	5 /	7
audav /	shadhav	5 /	6
audav /	audav	5 /	5

The Selection and Positioning of the Various Swaras

Various notes in the raag have a particular name or designation, based on their role in the raag.

The *vadi* swara is the particular swara that is most frequently used in a raag. In a raag, the vadi swara is comparable to "the king" of the swaras.

The *samvadi* swara is the second most frequently used swara in a particular raag. In relation to the king (vadi swara), the samvadi swara can be compared with the king's prime minister.

The *anuvadi* swaras are all the remaining swaras in a raag. In the analogy of the king and his kingdom, the anuvadi swaras can be compared to the subjects.

The *vivadi* swaras are those that cannot generally be used in a particular raag because they are dissonant or rather offensive to the ear. In the above mentioned king analogy, a vivadi swara is like an enemy or a foreigner, who needs to be avoided or watched diligently.

A *varjita* swara is a swara which cannot be used in a raag at any cost. The difference between a *varjita* and *vivadi* swara is that expert musicians can carefully use a vivadi swara and thereby enhance the beauty and sweetness of a given raag. However, the use of a varjita swara in a particular raag is completely forbidden and impossible, even to adept musicians.

The Pakar

Often, it is possible for someone familiar with a melody to identify that melody when only a few notes have been sung. In a similar way, raags can also be identified from just a few notes. The *pakar* is the most succinct arrangement of those swaras and also the minimum number of swaras that must be sung to identify the raag.

Samaya

Indian music is unique because it takes into account the psychological effect of music on the mind at different times of the day and night. There is always an appropriate time to sing or play a particular raag; a time when it will be most effective. This is called *raag samaya,* or the hour of the raag. Singing a raag at another time would not produce so appropriate an emotional or psychological state.

Purvanga and Uttranga: The Parts of the Scale

The saptak or scale can be divided into two parts. These two parts are what are called in the West, the tetrachords.

The *purvanga* swaras are: sa, re, ga, ma.

The *uttranga* swaras are: pa, dha, ni, (sa).

A raag that has its vadi swara in the lower tetrachord is called a *purva raag.* One that has its vadi swara in the upper tetrachord is called an *uttara raag.*

The Performance of a Raag

During the performance of a raag, the performer makes use of many vocal devices and techniques to make the presentation pleasing to his or her listeners. Among these are the following three skills:

Kana swara: The use of "grace notes." This is the act of lightly touching upon a preceding or successive swara in the act of playing or singing the main one.

Khataka-murki: When three swaras are sung together in a rapid, circular motion it is called a *khataka.* Doing the same process with four or five swaras is called a *murki.*

Meend (portamento): When a musician gracefully and tastefully slides through all the swaras of an interval (for example, from sa to pa) in an uninterrupted flow, that is called *meend.*

These vocal techniques are used by skilled vocalists to enhance the raag. They require that the performer have great control and artistry in the use of his or her voice.

Avayava

Avayava literally means a limb or part, which here refers to the parts of a song. In the ancient system of singing, there used to be four parts: *sthayi,* (permanent or main chorus or melody), *antara* (refrain or variation), *sanchari,* and *abhoga.* The modern system of singing, however, consists for the most part of only two limbs: *sthayi* (chorus) and *antara* (verse). In some of the ancient singing styles like *dhrupad,* however, one can find all four parts of a song even today. (Dhrupad is a special and very ancient style of singing where each syllable of each word is broken down and sung individually.)

Alaap

When a musician performs a raag, at the very beginning, before the actual composition itself, he or she presents the swaras of the raag in a slow tempo and contemplative mood. This is called the *alaap.* During the alaap, the performer may make use of all of the performance techniques listed above. The alaap is considered by many musicians to be the most difficult part of a performance to do well. It calls upon the meditative qualities as well as the musicianship of the performer.

Taan

When the performer sings clusters of swaras in a raag in a rapid tempo, the process is called *taan.* Through taan, the musician expands the raag. Many of the taans are derived from etude-like works called *alankars,* which are discussed briefly below. Taans also required great skill and vocal control of the performer.

Matra and Taal

The Sanskrit word *matra* is related to the English word "meter." In music, both words are used in reference to the time element of a piece, its rhythm. A matra is the smallest unit of the measurement of time—a micro-moment or a beat.

INDIAN MUSIC

The pattern of matras or beats which forms what in Western music is actually the meter is called the *taal* of a piece in Indian music. There are many different taals, and each taal or rhythmic pattern is named. Thus, the taal that corresponds in some ways to the meter 16/4 in Western music is called *teentaal;* the taal corresponding to 6/3 time is *dadra.* But in Indian rhythmic structure there also exist a number of subtle elements that are not commonly found in the West. A taal or pattern consists of four main components: *vibhag, tali, khali,* and *sam.* When this entire structure of the taal is organized for performance, it is technically called the *theka.*

To illustrate the four components, we will consider one of the basic Indian taals, teentaal. Teentaal has sixteen matras (or beats) existing in its pattern.

1	2	3	4	5	6	7	8	9	10	11	12	13	14	15	16
x				2				0				3			
sam				vibhag				khali							

This particular taal, teentaal, is divided into four sections. Each section is called *vibhag,* and in this taal each vibhag contains four matras, or beats, for the total of sixteen shown in the diagram. The vertical lines demarcate the sections. Generally, the first matra or beat of the taal, which is usually the strongest matra rhythmically, is called *sam.* The sam is indicated on the diagram by an 'x.' The weakest matra in the taal is called *khali,* and it is indicated in the notation with a '0.' Finally, while counting or singing, the performer makes a clap of the hands on the strong matra, or sam, and on the first matra of subsequent vibhags, except for the khali vibhag. This clap is called tali.

Lay (Tempo)

A taal can be played at a variety of tempos. The tempo is the speed at which the taal is played and is called the *lay.* There are three main divisions of lay: *vilambit* (slow), *madhya* (medium), and *drut* (fast).

Alankar (Etude)

A systematic arrangement of varnas that help a student to develop technical ability is called an *alankar.* The practice of alankars is of utmost importance in order to prepare a good foundation for performance. The thirty alankars or exercises given in Chapter Three are first practiced in bilawal thaat and then in each of the other ten thaats. By practicing these alankars, a student both cultures his voice and trains his fingers on his instrument. This practice is a wonderful preparation for performance and thoroughly imbues the mind of the performer with the various combinations of swaras. The exercises given should be systematically and regularly practiced, following the guidelines given in that chapter.

Thus, at this point, we have reviewed the basic terminology of Indian music. You may need to review and study this chapter several times to thoroughly integrate an understanding of these terms. While the terms may initially seem a little foreign or difficult, you will find that your understanding develops quickly as you study and practice.

CHAPTER TWO

VOICE TRAINING TECHNIQUES

In this next section I am going to explain a comprehensive method of developing and training your voice that is both reliable and beneficial. This technique will be helpful to anyone who wishes to speak clearly or to enjoy the practical art of singing. Using this method of practice systematically every day will definitely result in improvement in the beauty and clarity of one's voice. I want to make clear from the beginning that no one should ever feel that his or her voice is bad and cannot be trained for music. Any voice can benefit from this training. Actually, what needs to be trained is your sense of hearing. It is true, as the Bible says, that "when you have an ear to hear, you hear."

There are two major sensory systems in the human being—the auditory system and the visual system—which are somewhat like two types of personalities. In order to sing, the auditory system needs to have perfect coordination. The effective expression of the auditory system requires that the areas of the ears, nose, and throat be in good condition. If you have any illness or physical difficulty in these areas that affects the voice, then a medical specialist in this field may be able to help. In other cases, when distress or difficulty in using the voice is caused by tension or misuse, then a good music teacher is the answer.

In India, a folk story is told about a donkey and a jackal who secretly managed to break into a farmer's field to eat his crops at night. For many nights they enjoyed plundering the farmer's produce and each time, they disappeared by morning. But one night, the donkey became especially happy with his good fortune and declared that he wished to sing a song to express his great joy at his delicious meal. The jackal, not trusting the donkey's voice, tried to talk him out of it. The donkey responded boastfully, "I know how to sing; I know about the seven swaras, the twenty-two shrutis, and all the rules of composition! Who do you think you are talking to?"

At that the donkey began to sing, and the jackal quietly ran away and hid. Of course, after only a few notes of the donkey's voice, the farmer was alerted to the donkey's presence in the field and came running. He beat the donkey and hung a heavy rock around his neck to keep him from further mischief. Thus, the donkey learned that music theory alone is not enough to make one into a musician.

This lesson can be applied by beginning students. Music is a field of knowledge that really requires genuine self-training, not mere intellectual knowledge. If you want to make progress, choose a teacher who truly likes to teach—not someone whose greed or fanaticism lead him to have a narrow or academic approach to music. Remember that the choice of your teacher is important, because music is really learned from a teacher rather than through books.

Techniques for Practicing Vocal Music

To begin to develop your vocal practice, rise during the early hours of the morning and, after finishing your ablutions, drink two large glasses of tea-hot fresh lemon water. This drink will help to cleanse your system and to establish a regular cycle of evacuation of the bowels. This will help you to feel light, alert, and energetic prior to singing.

When you are ready to begin your singing practice, sit in a comfortable, steady posture. You should face either east, north or west but not toward the south. The reason for sitting facing in these directions has to do with the natural polarity of the body. Over time, those sensitive to this polarity will feel the difference and will understand why sitting toward the south is not recommended.

In your sitting posture, your spine should be balanced and erect, so that you can breathe freely and diaphragmatically.

There are vast differences between the practice of Indian music and Western vocal music. One apparently simple divergence (that actually has very profound effects) is that Western music is mainly sung in a standing position, while Indian music is always sung sitting down. This difference in position is very important. In order to concentrate on the subtle aspects of the voice, the physical position must be stable, relaxed, and balanced. Sitting quietly in a relaxed, comfortable position is thought to be best for this type of concentration.

After learning to sit comfortably, you must next establish the habit of good breathing. Proper breathing is the basis of good singing. In order to gain control of your respiratory process and maintain a feeling of relaxation at the same time, you need to practice diaphragmatic breathing. The diaphragm is one of the strongest muscles in the body. It is located just beneath the lungs and divides the torso into two parts, an upper and a lower section. The upper section contains the lungs and heart. The lower section contains all the abdominal organs. In order to breathe deeply and in a relaxed manner, you need to learn to use your diaphragm muscle in order to allow the lungs to expand fully. This is the most efficient and by far the healthiest way of breathing. Diaphragmatic breathing allows one to develop control of the voice.

Developing Diaphragmatic Breathing

A competent teacher will show you first how to practice diaphragmatic breathing in a number of postures. The easiest posture for beginners is the yoga posture called "crocodile pose." To assume this posture, lie on your stomach with your legs relaxed and your toes turned either in or out. Bring your arms above your shoulders as pictured below, and rest your forehead on your forearms or hands, whichever is more comfortable. Once you are settled in the posture, let your body rest and begin to feel the gentle rhythm of your own breathing. you will find that as you inhale, your lower back slowly rises, and as you exhale, your back will gently lower. As you bring your awareness to the sides of the body and to the navel region, you will find that these areas are expanding with each inhalation and contracting as you exhale. These are the signs of diaphragmatic breathing. During this practice, as with all normal breathing, you should breathe only through your nose and not through your mouth. Let your breath become deep, smooth, and even. Let the length of the inhalations and exhalations be equal.

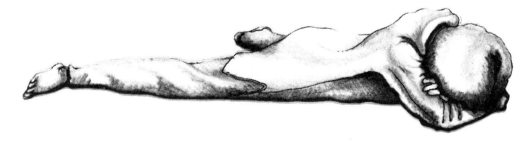

Crocodile Pose

To learn to deepen the breath, let your breath flow out a little more than usual for a few exhalations. Then, simply relax and let your body expand as you inhale. Your breath will become very deep. You need not try to breathe artificially. After a few breaths in which the exhalation is expanded in this way, go back to a normal breathing pattern, continuing to unblock your breath by relaxing on the inhalations. You will find that your breath has naturally become a little deeper and more complete.

Next, pay attention to the pause between the exhalation and inhalation. Ideally, the breath should be without any pauses. Pauses interrupt the steady flow of breathing and damage the nervous system. They are related to many sorrows, including negative thinking. At the end of your inhalation, simply relax again, and the exhalation will begin. By relaxing completely, you can let each breath flow into the next breath.

To develop your voice, you must establish deep, diaphragmatic breathing as your normal breathing style. In order to do this, you should first practice the crocodile breathing exercise three times each day for ten minutes. It will take only a matter of weeks before you notice that your regular breathing pattern has become serene, even, and deep.

Continue to practice diaphragmatic breathing in other postures, both sitting and lying down. After the habit has become firmly established, you can gradually begin to lengthen the duration of the exhalation. Eventually you can establish the ratio of 2:1 Breathing—that is, the length of the exhalation should be twice that of the inhalation. When you do 2:1 Breathing, make sure your breathing remains comfortable and you do not go beyond your comfortable capacity. This process should be gradually developed over an entire year's time. There is no hurry; if you expand the exhalation slowly then you will not damage the tissues of the lungs. Eventually, an exhalation of up to one full minute in duration can be mastered. This mastery of complete exhalation is helpful for cleansing and purifying the lungs and body tissues, and will provide the foundation for good breath control during singing.

There are also other breathing exercises that you should learn, including Alternate Nostril Breathing (Nadi Shodhanam), the Bellows breathing exercise (Bhastrika), and a special yoga breathing technique called *Ujjayi*. All these should be learned from a competent teacher. In themselves, these exercises have marvelous qualities and can make the voice very melodious. The text *Science of Breath,* which is available through the Himalayan Institute, will prove very helpful in understanding this aspect of vocal training and will give you many useful instructions on relaxed, diaphragmatic breathing.

One special method of breathing that is not mentioned in books was taught to me by my first music teacher, Sri Mukerjee of Calcutta. He had a wonderful and melodious voice and could sing notes from a range of four octaves without difficulty. He showed me how to breathe both from the mouth and the nose at the same time during singing. This skill, however is only possible, and can only be done properly, after practicing the preparatory exercises given above. When you develop that special technique of exhaling and inhaling through both mouth and nose, then you can sing for many hours without fatigue. This practice should always be done in a sitting posture and not while lying, standing or walking about.

Vocal Exercises One and Two

The next step in your program of voice training is to begin to practice humming. There is a particular technique of humming that should be done correctly. As you hum, the proper vowel to think of is the vowel "a," as in "along." This will produce a round, full, humming sound. Sometimes students develp a bad habit of mentally hearing a long "a" sound or the nasal sound, "an," as they hum. Neither of these sounds will help you to develop your voice as effectively as the sound "a."

There are two types of humming exercises that you should practice. They are both variations on a practice called *Brahmari,* or "the sound of the bee." In the first exercise, practice making a humming sound in your normal voice range, as you exhale. This humming will resemble the sound of the "male" bee. During this practice, concentrate on the area of the epiglottis and you will find that you can produce a sound surprisingly like a bee. Practice making this humming sound for ten minutes. After completing this exercise, let your voice rise until you are producing a high pitched sound, the sound of a "female" bee. Again, practice this higher sound for ten minutes. You will be happily surprised to learn that Brahmari is a very powerful form of therapy and a cure for many kinds of sinus problems, especially when it is combined with medical care from your doctor. Sinusitis, sore throats, and moisture or wax in the ears can all change the quality of the voice, and the practice of Brahmari is particularly helpful to singers, because it helps to eliminate these problems.

25

INDIAN MUSIC

Practicing Swaras

Now you are ready to begin vocalizing the swaras or syllables that will lead to performing raags and other melodies of Indian music. In Indian music, two aspects of music, "singing and swinging," go hand in hand; one is not really complete without the other. The origin of singing is in the swaras, and the origin of "swinging," or rhythm, is the *taal*. The taal is not merely the beat or measurement— it is actually the pulsations of sound that make the rhythm itself pleasant. There are many different taals, or beats, and students should learn to practice taals or rhythm before starting to sing melodies. Both swara and taal should be practiced side by side. Together, they form the foundation of Indian music.

One common problem in the beginning of the study of Indian music is that the subtlety of the swaras can be lost if the student does not learn to pay close attention to good intonation. In India, the various timbres of sound were divided into five categories. There are: (1) sounds produced by strings, (2) sounds produced by wind instruments, (3) sounds of leather drums, (4) sounds of other metal or wood percussion instruments, and finally (5) the human voice. Of these categories of sound, only strings, wind instruments, and the human voice have the potential range and subtlety to produce the full gamut of swaras. Recently, the harmonium and the piano have been added to Indian music performances. While certainly capable of producing many of the swaras, these two instruments are unfortunately limited in their ability to adjust to the subtle nuances of intonation necessary for the fullest and deepest musical expression. If you feel that your ear or your sound discrimination is very untrained, then in the beginning, you can use the piano or harmonium to get started. In careful vocal training, however, students should learn to listen to themselves closely and attentively and to train their ear to the accompaniment of a string instrument. A simple method of doing this is to first make a tape recording of a *tanpura,* an Indian string instrument that is used to play the harmonious drone sounds that accompany all musical performances. The common tuning of the tanpura produces the sounds *pa, sa, sa, sa ,* that help to keep your voice in harmony. Then, you can do your vocal exercises with this drone playing quietly in the background. This will be very helpful for you and will save you the wasted effort of practicing with instruments such as the piano or harmonium that only dull your sense of intonation.

Vocal exercises must always begin on a particular swara. Sometimes teachers recommend beginning with vocalizing the lowest note of the three main saptaks (or octaves). This note is called *shadaj.* However, I don't recommend that students practice producing the lowest swara, shadaj, if they are young. This lowest note should be practiced only after one is forty years of age. Through the practice of the swara shadaj, the highest notes of the upper octave are also mastered. Shadaj is considered to be the mother of all sounds or swaras, and that is why highly proficient and skilled musicians learn to apply shadaj well.

Morning Practice

More commonly, vocal practice is begun on the *sa* of the madhya (middle) saptak (corresponding to the range of the Western middle c). This *sa* is established at one's own proper place by using three swaras: *sa, re,* and *ni* just below *sa.* (That is, the *ni* of the mandra, or lowest, saptak.) First, begin by singing the following variations for a few minutes, using the shuddh (pure) tones of the natural seven-note scale:

(1) sa - re - sa
(2) sa - re - ni - sa
(3) ni - sa - re - sa
(4) re - sa - ni - sa
(5) re - re - sa - sa - ni - ni - sa - sa

Next, descend slowly from *sa* down into the mandra (lower) saptak. Go down to *ga* if possible, otherwise descend at least to *ma* . Do not overstretch your voice in the mandra saptak if you are young or are just beginning your training.

Each saptak contains seven swaras, and the upper *sa* makes the eighth swara. As we noted earlier, these eight swaras are divided into two parts, the lower and upper tetrachords. The lower tetrachord is *sa, re, ga,* and *ma,* and the upper tetrachord is *pa, dha, ni,* and *sa* . In order to practice the full range of swaras, students should practice ascending in the middle (madhya) saptak as well as descending into mandra saptak. One should perfect the purvanga (lower) part first, then the uttranga (upper), and then both together. Then you can begin to sing upwards from *sa* through the entire madhya saptak, and also go downward from *sa* into the mandra saptak as far as comfortable for your voice at this time.

Two Methods of Practicing Scales

While you practice singing scales you can use your voice to vocalize in two ways: you can sing the name of the tone (such as *sa* or *re* or *ga*), or you can sing one of twelve vowels. These twelve sounds are as follows:

short a	short u	long ae
long a	long u	long o
short i	short ri	long au
long i	long e	nasal am (or om)

To use these vowel sounds for each swara that you practice, sing each vowel.

As you have already learned, the musical scale has two forms: the "natural" scale of seven pure notes, and the chromatic scale (including sharps and flats) with twelve notes. After an initial period of three months, in which you practice the basic breathing exercises, humming, and the seven shuddh swaras, you will then be ready to go on to the next stage of systematic practice. At this point, you can gradually expand your exercises to all twelve notes of the chromatic scale. When you have practiced the above exercises regularly and faithfully for three months, some of the benefits that you will have already experienced should include:

1. Your vocal range will have become expanded,
2. Your voice will have become round and melodious, and
3. You will have developed the ability to sing without exertion.

The next stage of practice will give you a comprehensive knowledge of both swara and matra (beat). As you do these exercises, you will continue to observe positive changes in your voice.

In the following exercise, again begin to sing the tones of the scale, either upward in the madhya saptak, or downward into the mandra saptak. This time, as you sing, repeat rhythmically *in your mind* the syllable that you are vocalizing externally. Practice both the names of the swaras and the vowel sounds of the alphabet. Repeat these sounds in your mind rhythmically twelve times each, as if you were counting from one to twelve. Go through the entire scale, in two ways— first ascending and then descending, and secondly descending first and then ascending. Do this whole practice counting each swara and vowel. Next, do the same exercises with eleven repetitions. Then, practice the repetitions ten times, decreasing successively to nine, eight, seven, so on, and eventually coming down to one repetition. Then, work back upwards from one repetition to twelve repetitions again. This counting exercise should be done in the vilambit (slow) tempo—

about the speed of the beating of your heart. This is a unique method of culturing and strengthening your voice and training yourself in matra, and it is a preparation for learning taal.

Alternate Practice Exercise

The main purpose of this morning practice is voice culture and development. The voice is cultured by practicing *sa* (the first note in the saptak), but by using the sound "a" rather than the actual *sa*. The vowel "a" is pronounced as "au" in the word "author." Next, the same tone should be practiced with the vowel "i" which is similar to the sound "ee" as in "meet." Each of these vowels should be practiced on long tones ten or twenty times each.

Next, practice the note *pa* (the fifth note in the saptak) while using the same "a," "i," and "u" sounds, for six long tones.

Continue the exercises, practicing *ma, ga,* and *re* (the fourth, third, and second notes of the saptak) using "a" for one minute with each note.

The Practice of Shadaj

Practice *sa,* the first note of the lowest scale, for approximately fifteen to twenty minutes. This *sa* also should be practiced for five months regularly only with "a." Remember that young people should be careful not to strain their voices while attempting to reach *sa* and the lower notes.

After five months of this practice, one should incorporate "i," "u," and finally "om," and practice them using shadaj, as well. When you practice "a," "i," "u," and "om" in the lowest scale, wait approximately thirty minutes before practicing alankars.

Important Guidelines

While practicing Indian music, pay close attention to the following suggestions:

(1) Practice before a mirror so that you are conscious of your facial expressions and can eliminate facial tension as well as unnecessary gestures made with your hands and feet. The mouth should be opened the proper distance. To determine this, a beginning student should be able to insert the thumb and index

finger about one inch into the mouth when they are pinched together. This is the proper distance for the mouth to be open during swara sadhana. The sound produced should be round and seem to have a circular motion. The sound should not be annoying, harsh or shrill.

(2) Sing only as long as you can comfortably, and go only as far as you can comfortably in the lower saptak. Do not force your voice to the end of either the taar saptak, or the lowest saptak. Do not let your voice become nasal. Keep your voice rounded, and do not allow it to hiss.

(3) Wait for at least thirty minutes to an hour after a meal before beginning your practice. As an aid to swara sadhana, some breathing exercises (such as breath retention according to one's capacity) can be very helpful.

(4) The tape recorder can be an invaluable instrument to aid in your practice. Tape your practice sessions and then listen to your tape to identify and learn to correct your mistakes.

(5) Present your practice material to your teacher every six to eight weeks so that any necessary corrections can be made and you will continue to improve.

(6) One important guideline for this stage of practice is to pay careful attention to the way that your voice moves from one swara to the next. The method to practice, both ascending and descending, is to "slide" the voice gently and gracefully from one note to the next without breaking the sound of your voice. This method of movement from swara to swara touches upon all the shrutis lying between the notes, and gives an artistic impression of fullness. In addition, the movement has a smoothness that is pleasing to the ear. Care in practicing this will soon make your voice melodious and beautiful. If you find your voice tiring, or your mind repeatedly fails to sing the correct swara, then stop practicing. It is of little use to go on singing when you are tired. Singers and public speakers both will find it beneficial to reduce casual, unnecessary speaking in order to save their voices.

(7) Once you have learned to use the swaras appropriately, practice the shuddh swaras in the morning, and in the evening practice both shuddh and vikrit swaras. Gradually, you can begin to add alankar exercises (given in Chapter

Three) to your evening practice. These should first be sung in a slow tempo, using the swaras of bilawal thaat. Then, practice the alankars using each of the other nine thaats. You will soon learn to recognize whether you are singing the correct swara or not. When you begin to recognize and notice your own mistakes you actually are making progress. Realizing one's mistakes is a reminder not to repeat them again.

(8) Any student who practices these exercises daily for forty-five minutes to one hour for a period of three months, will be amazed to see the difference in his or her voice. Then, for more information regarding voice training and music therapy, write directly to the School of Eastern Music of the Himalayan Institute.

CHAPTER THREE

THIRTY ALANKARS
TO PRACTICE

The following vocal exercises serve two important purposes. They root and establish the swaras (notes) in the mind of the singer so that the precise pitch and the swara names become second nature. The exercises are also inserted, either in whole or in part, into actual performances. The practice of the triangular alankars (exercises) begins at the top. Pay particular attention to whether the exercise is ascending or descending. Each alankar must be practiced:

a) slowly
b) using the names of the swara syllables
c) using the vowels of the alphabet
d) using the swaras of each of the ten thaats
e) many times

Alankars

1. **aroh:**

                              sa
                           sa re sa
                        sa re ga re sa
                     sa re ga ma ga re sa
                  sa re ga ma pa ma ga re sa
               sa re ga ma pa dha pa ma ga re sa
            sa re ga ma pa dha ni dha pa ma ga re sa
         sa re ga ma pa dha ni sa ni dha pa ma ga re sa

avaroh:

                                        sá

                                 sá ni sá

                           sá ni dha ni sá

                     sá ni dha pa dha ni sá

                sá ni dha pa ma pa dha ni sá

            sá ni dha pa ma ga ma pa dha ni sá

       sá ni dha pa ma ga re ga ma pa dha ni sá

   sá ni dha pa ma ga re sa re ga ma pa dha ni sá

2. **aroh:**   sa sa, re re, ga ga, ma ma, pa pa, dha dha, ni ni, sá sá

     avaroh: sá sá, ni ni, dha dha, pa pa, ma ma, ga ga, re re, sa sa

3. **aroh:**   sa sa sa, re re re, ga ga ga, ma ma ma, pa pa pa, dha dha dha, ni ni ni, sá sá sá

     avaroh: sá sá sá, ni ni ni, dha dha dha, pa pa pa, ma ma ma, ga ga ga, re re re, sa sa sa

4. **aroh:**   sa re ga, re ga ma, ga ma pa, ma pa dha, pa dha ni, dha ni sá

     avaroh: sá ni dha, ni dha pa, dha pa ma, pa ma ga, ma ga re, ga re sa

5. **aroh:**   sa re ga ma, re ga ma pa, ga ma pa dha, ma pa dha ni, pa dha ni sá

     avaroh: sá ni dha pa, ni dha pa ma, dha pa ma ga, pa ma ga re, ma ga re sa

6. **aroh:**   sa re ga ma pa, re ga ma pa dha, ga ma pa dha ni, ma pa dha ni sá

     avaroh: sá ni dha pa ma, ni dha pa ma ga, dha pa ma ga re, pa ma ga re sa

7. **aroh:**   sa re ga ma pa dha, re ga ma pa dha ni, ga ma pa dha ni sá

avaroh: sā ni dha pa ma ga, ni dha pa ma ga re, dha pa ma ga re sa

8. **aroh:** sa re sa re ga, re ga re ga ma, ga ma ga ma pa, ma pa ma pa dha, pa dha pa dha ni, dha ni dha ni sā

    avaroh: sā ni sā ni dha, ni dha ni dha pa, dha pa dha pa ma, pa ma pa ma ga, ma ga ma ga re, ga re ga re sa

9. **aroh:** sa re sa re ga ma, re ga re ga ma pa, ga ma ga ma pa dha, ma pa ma pa dha ni, pa dha pa dha ni sā

    avaroh: sā ni sā ni dha pa, ni dha ni dha pa mā, dha pa dha pa ma ga, pa ma pa ma ga re, ma ga ma ga re sa

10. **aroh:** sa ga, re ma, ga pa, ma dha, pa ni, dha sā

    avaroh: sā dha, ni pa, dha ma, pa ga, ma re, ga sa

11. **aroh:** sa sa ga ga, re re ma ma, ga ga pa pa, ma ma dha dha, pa pa ni ni, dha dha sā sā

    avaroh: sā sā dha dha, ni ni pa pa, dha dha ma ma, pa pa ga ga, ma ma re re, ga ga sa sa

12. **aroh:** sa ma, re pa, ga dha, ma ni, pa sā

    avaroh: sā pa, ni ma, dha ga, pa re, ma sa

13. **aroh:** sa sa ma ma, re re pa pa, ga ga dha dha, ma ma ni ni, pa pa sā sā

    avaroh: sā sā pa pa, ni ni ma ma, dha dha ga ga, pa pa re re, ma ma sa sa

14. **aroh:** sa pa, re dha, ga ni, ma sā

    avaroh: sā ma, ni ga, dha re, pa sa

15. **aroh:** sa sa pa pa, re re dha dha, ga ga ni ni, ma ma sā sā

avaroh: sȧ sȧ ma ma, ni ni ga ga, dha dha re re, pa pa sa sa

16. **aroh:** ga re sa, ma ga re, pa ma ga, dha pa ma, ni dha pa, sȧ ni dha, rė sȧ ni, gȧ rė sȧ

    avaroh: dha ni sȧ, pa dha ni, ma pa dha, ga ma pa, re ga ma, sa re ga, ni̠ sa re, dha ni̠ sa

17. **aroh:** sa re sa re ga re, re ga re ga ma ga, ga ma ga ma pa ma, ma pa ma pa dha pa, pa dha pa dha ni dha, dha ni dha ni sȧ ni, ni sȧ ni sȧ rė sȧ

    avaroh: sȧ ni sȧ ni dha ni, ni dha ni dha pa dha, dha pa dha pa ma pa, pa ma pa ma ga ma, ma ga ma ga re ga, ga re ga re sa re, re sa re sa ni̠ sa

18. **aroh:** sa re ga re sa, re ga ma ga re, ga ma pa ma ga, ma pa dha pa ma, pa dha ni dha pa, dha ni sȧ ni dha, ni sȧ rė sȧ ni, sȧ rė gȧ rė sȧ

    avaroh: sȧ ni dha ni sȧ, ni dha pa dha ni, dha pa ma pa dha, pa ma ga ma pa, ma ga re ga ma, ga re sa re ga, re sa ni̠ sa re, sa ni̠ dha ni̠ sa

19. **aroh:** sa re ga ma ga re sa, re ga ma pa ma ga re, ga ma pa dha pa ma ga, ma pa dha ni dha pa ma, pa dha ni sȧ ni dha pa, dha ni sȧ rė sȧ ni dha, ni sȧ rė gȧ rė sȧ ni, sȧ rė gȧ mȧ gȧ rė sȧ

    avaroh: sȧ ni dha pa dha ni sȧ, ni dha pa ma pa dha ni, dha pa ma ga ma pa dha, pa ma ga re ga ma pa, ma ga re sa re ga ma, ga re sa ni̠ sa re ga, re sa ni̠ dha ni̠ sa re, sa ni̠ dha pa dha ni̠ sa

20. **aroh:** sa re ga ma pa ma ga re sa, re ga ma pa dha pa ma ga re, ga ma pa dha ni dha pa ma ga, ma pa dha ni sȧ ni dha pa ma, pa dha ni sȧ rė sȧ ni dha pa, dha ni sȧ rė gȧ rė sȧ ni dha, ni sȧ rė gȧ mȧ gȧ rė sȧ ni, sȧ rė gȧ mȧ pȧ mȧ gȧ rė sȧ

    avaroh: sȧ ni dha pa ma pa dha ni sȧ, ni dha pa ma ga ma pa dha ni, dha pa ma ga re ga ma pa dha, pa ma ga re sa re ga ma pa, ma ga re

sa ni sa re ga ma, ga re sa ni dha ni sa re ga, re sa ni dha pa dha
ni sa re, sa ni dha pa ma pa dha ni sa

21. **aroh:**   sa re ga sa re, re ga ma re ga, ga ma pa ga ma, ma pa dha ma pa,
pa dha ni pa dha, dha ni sa dha ni, ni sa re ni sa

     avaroh: sa ni dha sa ni, ni dha pa ni dha, dha pa ma dha pa, pa ma ga pa
ma, ma ga re ma ga, ga re sa ga re, re sa ni re sa

22. **aroh:**   sa ga re sa, re ma ga re, ga pa ma ga, ma dha pa ma, pa ni dha
pa, dha sa ni dha, ni re sa ni, sa ga re sa

     avaroh: sa dha ni sa, ni pa dha ni, dha ma pa dha, pa ga ma pa, ma re ga
ma, ga sa re ga, re ni sa re, sa dha ni sa

23. **aroh:**   sa re ni sa, re ga sa re, ga ma re ga, ma pa ga ma, pa dha ma pa,
dha ni pa dha, ni sa dha ni, sa re ni sa

     avaroh: sa ni re sa, ni dha sa ni, dha pa ni dha, pa ma dha pa, ma ga pa
ma, ga re ma ga, re sa ga re, sa ni re sa

24. **aroh:**   sa ma re ga, re pa ga ma, ga dha ma pa, ma ni pa dha, pa sa dha
ni, dha re ni sa

     avaroh: sa pa ni dha, ni ma dha pa, dha ga pa ma, pa re ma ga, ma sa ga
re, ga ni re sa

25. **aroh:**   sa pa re ma, re dha ga pa, ga ni ma dha, ma sa pa ni, pa re dha sa

     avaroh: sa ma ni pa, ni ga dha ma, dha re pa ga, pa sa ma re, ma ni ga sa

26. **aroh:**   sa re, sa ga, sa ma, sa pa, sa dha, sa ni, sa sa

     avaroh: sa ni, sa dha, sa pa, sa ma, sa ga, sa re, sa sa

27. **aroh:**   sa sa re re re, ga ga ma ma ma, pa pa dha dha dha, ni ni sa sa sa

avaroh: saˈ saˈ ni ni ni, dha dha pa pa pa, ma ma ga ga ga, re re sa sa sa

28. **aroh:** sa sa sa re re re re, ga ga ga ma ma ma ma, pa pa pa dha dha dha dha, ni ni ni saˈ saˈ saˈ saˈ

avaroh: saˈ saˈ saˈ ni ni ni ni, dha dha dha pa pa pa pa, ma ma ma ga ga ga ga, re re re sa sa sa sa

29. **aroh:** sa sa sa ga ga re re sa sa, re re re ma ma ga ga re re, ga ga ga pa pa ma ma ga ga, ma ma ma dha dha pa pa ma ma, pa pa pa ni ni dha dha pa pa, dha dha dha saˈ saˈ ni ni dha dha, ni ni ni reˈ reˈ saˈ saˈ ni ni, saˈ saˈ saˈ gaˈ gaˈ reˈ reˈ saˈ saˈ

avaroh: saˈ saˈ saˈ dha dha ni ni saˈ saˈ, ni ni ni pa pa dha dha ni ni, dha dha dha ma ma pa pa dha dha, pa pa pa ga ga ma ma pa pa, ma ma ma re re ga ga ma ma, ga ga ga sa sa re re ga ga, re re re ni ni sa sa re re, sa sa sa dha dha ni ni sa sa

30. **aroh:** sa sa sa re sa re re sa sa, re re re ga re ga ga re re, ga ga ga ma ga ma ma ga ga, ma ma ma pa ma pa pa ma ma, pa pa pa dha pa dha dha pa pa, dha dha dha ni dha ni ni dha dha, ni ni ni saˈ ni saˈ saˈ ni ni, saˈ saˈ saˈ reˈ saˈ reˈ reˈ saˈ saˈ

avaroh: saˈ saˈ saˈ ni saˈ ni ni saˈ saˈ, ni ni ni dha ni dha dha ni ni, dha dha dha pa dha pa pa dha dha, pa pa pa ma pa ma ma pa pa, ma ma ma ga ma ga ga ma ma, ga ga ga re ga re re ga ga, re re re sa ni sa sa re re, sa sa sa ni sa ni ni sa sa

THIRTY ALANKARS TO PRACTICE

अलंकार

१. आरोह-

सा

सा रे सा

सा रे ग रे सा

सा रे ग म ग रे सा

सा रे ग म प म ग रे सा

सा रे ग म प ध प म ग रे सा

सा रे ग म प ध नि ध प म ग रे सा

सा रे ग म प ध नि सां नि ध प म ग रे सा

अवरोह-

सां

सां नि सां

सां नि ध नि सां

सां नि ध प ध नि सां

सां नि ध प म प ध नि सां

सां नि ध प म ग म प ध नि सां

सां नि ध प म ग रे ग म प ध नि सां

सां नि ध प म ग रे सा रे ग म प ध नि सां

२. आरोह- सा सा, रे रे, ग ग, म म, प प, ध ध, नि नि, सां सां

अवरोह- सां सां, नि नि, ध ध, प प, म म, ग ग, रे रे, सा सा

३. आरोह- सा सा सा, रे रे रे, ग ग ग, म म म, प प प, ध ध ध, नि नि नि, सां सां सां

अवरोह- सां सां सां, नि नि नि, ध ध ध, प प प, म म म, ग ग ग, रे रे रे, सा सा सा

४. आरोह- सा रे ग, रे ग म, ग म प, म प ध, प ध नि, ध नि सां

39

अवरोह- सां नि ध, नि ध प, ध प म, प म ग, म ग रे, ग रे सा

५. आरोह- सा रे ग म, रे ग म प, ग म प ध, म प ध नि, प ध नि सां

अवरोह- सां नि ध प, नि ध प म, ध प म ग, प म ग रे, म ग रे सा

६. आरोह- सा रे ग म प, रे ग म प ध, ग म प ध नि, म प ध नि सां

अवरोह- सां नि ध प म, नि ध प म ग, ध प म ग रे, प म ग रे सा

७. आरोह- सा रे ग म प ध, रे ग म प ध नि, ग म प ध नि सां

अवरोह- सां नि ध प म ग, नि ध प म ग रे, ध प म ग रे सा

८. आरोह- सा रे सा रे ग, रे ग रे ग म, ग म ग म प, म प म प ध, प ध प ध नि, ध नि ध नि सां

अवरोह- सां नि सां नि ध, नि ध नि ध प, ध प ध प म, प म प म ग, म ग म ग रे, ग रे ग रे सा

९. आरोह- सा रे सा रे ग॰ म, रे ग रे ग म प, ग म ग म प ध, म प म प ध नि, प ध प ध नि सां

अवरोह- सां नि सा नि ध प, नि ध नि ध प म, ध प ध प म ग, प म प म ग रे, म ग म ग रे सा

१०. आरोह- सा ग, रे म, ग प, म ध, प नि, ध सां

अवरोह- सां ध, नि प, ध म, प ग, म रे, ग सा

११. आरोह- सा सा ग ग, रे रे म म, ग ग प प, म म ध ध, प प नि नि, ध ध सां सां

अवरोह- सां सां ध ध, नि नि प प, ध ध म म, प प ग ग, म म रे रे, ग ग सा सा

१२. आरोह- सा म, रे प, ग ध, म नि, प सां

अवरोह- सां प, नि म, ध ग, प रे, म सा

१३. आरोह- सा सा म म, रे रे प प, ग ग ध ध, म म नि नि, प प सां सां

अवरोह- सां सां प प, नि नि म म, ध ध ग ग, प प रे रे, म म सा सा

१४. आरोह- सा प, रे ध, ग नि, म सां

अवरोह- सां म, नि ग, ध रे, प सा

१५. आरोह- सा सा प प, रे रे ध ध, ग ग नि नि, म म सां सां

अवरोह- सां सां म म, नि नि ग ग, ध ध रे रे, प प सा सा

१६. आरोह- ग रे सा, म ग रे, प म ग, ध प म, नि ध प, सां नि ध, रें सां नि, गं रें सां

अवरोह- ध नि सां, प ध नि, म प ध, ग म प, रे ग म, सा रे ग, नि॒ सा रे, ध॒ नि॒ सा

१७. आरोह- सा रे सा रे ग रे, रे ग रे ग म ग, ग म ग म प म, म प म प ध प, प ध प ध नि ध, ध नि ध नि सां नि, नि सां नि सां रें सां

41

अवरोह- सां नि सां नि ध नि, नि ध नि ध प ध, ध प ध प म प, प म प म ग म, म ग
म ग रे ग, ग रे ग रे सा रे, रे सा रे सा नि॒ सा

१८. आरोह- सा रे ग रे सा, रे ग म ग रे, ग म प म ग, म प ध प म, प ध नि ध प, ध नि
सां नि ध, नि सां रें सां नि, सां रें गं रें सां

अवरोह- सां नि ध नि सां, नि ध प ध नि, ध प म प ध, प म ग म प, म ग रे ग म, ग रे
सा रे ग, रे सा नि॒ सा रे, सा नि॒ ध॒ नि॒ सा

१९. आरोह- सा रे ग म ग रे सा, रे ग म प म ग रे, ग म प ध प म ग, म प ध नि ध प म,
प ध नी सां नि ध प, ध नि सां रें सां नि ध, नि सां रें गं रें सां नि, सां रें गं मं गं
रें सां

अवरोह- सां नि ध प ध नि सां, नि ध प म प ध नि, ध प म ग म प ध, प म ग रे ग म
प, म ग रे सा रे ग म, ग रे सा नि॒ सा रे ग, रे सा नि॒ ध॒ नि॒ सा रे, सा नि॒ ध॒ प॒
ध॒ नि॒ सा

२०. आरोह- सा रे ग म प म ग रे सा, रे ग म प ध प म ग रे, ग म प ध नि ध प म ग, म प
ध नि सां नि ध प म, प ध नि सां रें सां नि ध प, ध नि सां रें गं रें सां नि ध, नि
सा रें गं मं गं रें सां नि, सां रें गं मं पं मं गं रें सां

अवरोह- सां नि ध प म प ध नि सां, नि ध प म ग म प ध नि, ध प म ग रे ग म प ध,
प म ग रे सा रे ग म प, म ग रे सा नि॒ सा रे ग म, ग रे सा नि॒ ध॒ नि॒ सा रे ग, रे
सा नि॒ ध॒ प॒ ध॒ नि॒ सा रे, सा नि॒ ध॒ प॒ म॒ प॒ ध॒ नि॒ सा

२१. आरोह- सा रे ग सा रे, रे ग म रे ग, ग म प ग म, म प ध म प, प ध नि प ध, ध नि
सां ध नि, नि सां रें नि सां

अवरोह- सां नि ध सां नि, नि ध प नि ध, ध प म ध प, प म ग प म, म ग रे म ग, ग रे
सा ग रे, रे सा नि॒ रे सा

२२. **आरोह-** सा ग रे सा, रे म ग रे, ग प म ग, म ध प म, प नि ध प, ध सां नि ध, नि रें
सां नि, सां गं रें सां

अवरोह- सां ध नि सां, नि प ध नि, ध म प ध, प ग म प, म रे ग म, ग सा रे ग, रे नि॒
सा रे, सा ध॒ नी॒ सा

२३. **आरोह-** सा रे नि॒ सा, रे ग सा रे, ग म रे ग, म प ग म, प ध म प, ध नि प ध, नि सां
ध नि, सां रें नि सां

अवरोह- सां नि रें सां, नि ध सां नि, ध प नि ध, प म ध प, म ग प म, ग रे म ग, रे सा
ग रे, सा नि॒ रे सा

२४. **आरोह-** सा म रे ग, रे प ग म, ग ध म प, म नि प ध, प सां ध नि, ध रें नि सां

अवरोह- सां प नि ध, नि म ध प, ध ग प म, प रे म ग, म सा ग रे, ग नि॒ रे सा

२५. **आरोह-** सा प रे म, रे ध ग प, ग नि म ध, म सां प नि, प रें ध सां

अवरोह- सां म नि प, नि ग ध म, ध रे प ग, प सा म रे, म नि॒ ग सा

२६. **आरोह-** सा रे, सा ग, सा म, सा प, सा ध, सा नि, सा सां

अवरोह- सां नि, सां ध, सां प, सां म, सां ग, सां रे, सां सा

२७. **आरोह-** सा सा रे रे रे, ग ग म म म, प प ध ध ध, नि नि सां सां सां

अवरोह- सां सां नि नि नि, ध ध प प प, म म ग ग ग, रे रे सा सा सा

२८. आरोह- सा सा सा रे रे रे रे, ग ग ग म म म म, प प प ध ध ध ध, नि नि नि सां सां सां सां

अवरोह- सां सां सां नि नि नि नि, ध ध ध प प प प, म म म ग ग ग ग, रे रे रे सा सा सा सा सा

२९. आरोह- सा सा सा ग ग रे रे सा सा, रे रे रे म म ग ग रे रे, ग ग ग प प म म ग ग, म म म ध ध प प म म, प प प नि नि ध ध प प, ध ध ध सां सां नि नि ध ध, नि नि नि रें रें सां सां नि नि, सां सां सां गं गं रें रें सां सां

अवरोह- सां सां सां ध ध ध नि नि सां सां, नि नि नि प प ध ध नि नि, ध ध ध म म प प ध ध, प प प ग ग म म प प, म म म रे रे ग ग म म, ग ग ग सा सा रे रे ग ग, रे रे रे नि॒ नि॒ सा सा रे रे, सा सा सा ध ध॒ नि॒ नि॒ सा सा

३०. आरोह- सा सा सा रे सा रे रे सा सा, रे रे रे ग रे ग ग रे रे, ग ग ग म ग म म ग ग, म म प म प प म म, प प प ध प ध प प, ध ध ध नि ध नि नि ध ध, नि नि नि सां नि सां सां नि नि, सां सां सां रें सां रें रें सां सां

अवरोह- सां सां सां नि सां नि नि सां सां, नि नि नि ध नि ध ध नि नि, ध ध ध प ध प प ध ध, प प प म प म म प प, म म म ग म ग ग म म, ग ग ग रे ग रे रे ग ग, रे रे रे सा नि॒ सा सा रे रे, सा सा सा नि॒ सा नि॒ नि॒ सा सा

CHAPTER FOUR

TEN CLASSICAL RAAGS

Raags (or ragas, as they are known in Sanskrit) are the classical musical forms of India that are probably best known in the West. These are traditional pieces that are sung or played at particular times of the day or night to create a certain mood or tone. Information about ten of the classical raags is summarized on the following pages. It would be impossible, without the guidance of a teacher, to create the sound of these raags merely from the printed information. Nonetheless, from these summaries you will find that you can gain a sense of how the different elements of Indian classical music come together in the form of an individual raag. You may need to refer to Chapter One in order to remember the meaning of the terms on these pages. A complete guide to Indian musical notation is found in Appendix B. [The beginning student should not expect to begin singing these raags, but rather, should begin with the exercises given in Chapter Two.]

You will note in the following pages that the ten classical raags are given along with their alaap, sthayi, and antara. For each raag, these are given first in English and then in Hindi script.

GURU VANDANA

(Raag Bilawal)   **(Kaherwa Taal)**

Gurur brahma gurur vishnuh, gurur devo mahesvarah,
Guruh saaksaat param brahma, tasmai sri gurave namah.

sthayi:

ga	ga	-	re	ma	ga	-	-	ga	ga	-	ma	pa	pa	-	-
gu	rur	ꜱ	bra	ꜱ	hmaa	ꜱ	ꜱ	gu	rur	ꜱ	vi	ꜱ	shnu	ꜱ	ꜱ
x				0				x				0			

dha	dha	-	dha	-	dha	-	-	pa	dhani	dhapa	ni	pa	-	-	-
gu	rur	ꜱ	de	ꜱ	vo	ꜱ	ꜱ	ma	heꜱ	ꜱꜱ	shva	rah	ꜱ	ꜱ	ꜱ
x				0				x				0			

antara:

pa	pa	-	sȧ	-	sȧ	-	sȧ	pa	dha	-	ma	ga	-	ga	-
gu	ruh	ꜱ	saa	ꜱ	ksa	ꜱ	at	pa	ra	ꜱ	m	bra	ꜱ	hma	ꜱ
x				0				x				0			

re	re	ga	ma	re	-	-	ga	ga	gama	pa	re	re	sa	-	-
ta	s	ma	i	sri	ꜱ	ꜱ	gu	ra	veꜱ	ꜱ	ꜱ	na	mah	ꜱ	ꜱ
x				0				x				0			

गुरु वन्दना

(राग बिलावल)   (ताल कहरवा)

गुरुर्ब्रह्मा गुरुर्विष्णु, गुरुर्देवो महेश्वरः।
गुरुःसाक्षात् परम ब्रह्म, तस्मै श्री गुरवे नमः।।

स्थाई-

ग	ग	-	रे	म	ग	-	-	ग	ग	-	म	प	प	-	-
गु	रु	ऽ	ब्र	ऽ	ह्मा	ऽ	ऽ	गु	रु	ऽ	र्वि	ऽ	ष्णु	ऽ	ऽ
x				o				x				o			

ध	ध	-	ध	-	ध	-	-	प	धनि	धप्	नि	प	-	-	-
गु	रु	ऽ	र्दे	ऽ	वो	ऽ	ऽ	म	हेऽ	ऽऽ	श्व	रः	ऽ	ऽ	ऽ
x				o				x				o			

अन्तरा-

प	प	-	सां	-	सां	-	सां	प	ध	-	म	ग	-	ग	-
गु	रुः	ऽ	सा	ऽ	क्षा	ऽ	त्	प	र	ऽ	म	ब्र	ऽ	ह्म	ऽ
x				o				x				o			

रे	रे	ग	म	रे	-	-	ग	ग	गम	प	रे	रे	सा	-	-
त	स्	म्	ऐ	श्री	ऽ	ऽ	गु	र	वे	ऽ	ऽ	न	मः	ऽ	ऽ
x				o				x				o			

ALHAIYA BILAWAL

thaat bilawal: sa re ga ma pa dha ni sa

swara: In this raag all shuddha (natural or pure) swaras are applied. During the avaroh (descending scale), komal ni is used along with dha. For example: dha ni dha pa

jati: shadav/sampurn   6/7

vadi swara: dha

samvadi swara: ga

time of singing: first part of the day

pakar: ga re ga pa ma ga ma re ga pa dha ni sa ni dha pa dha ni pa

aroh: sa re ga pa dha ni sa

avaroh: sa ni dha pa dha ni dha pa ma ga re sa

alaap:

1. sa S S S ^{sa}ga S S S ga ma re S S S sa S S S S S saresani dha S S S ni S S S ^{sa}ni sa S S S S

2. sa S S S ga S S S re ga S S S pa S S S ^{pa}ma S S ga S S S ga ma S S S re S S sa re ga S S S pa S S S dha S S S ni dha
   pa S S ga pa ma S S S ga ma re S S S ga pa S S S S dha ni S S dha pa S S S ma S S S ga ma re S S S S sa S S S S

3. sa re S S ga S S S ga pa S S S dha S S S ni S S S S sa S S S saresani dha S S pa S S S dha ni dha S S pa S S S ma
   ga ma re S S ga pa S S ma ga S S S S ^{ga}ma re S S sa S S

4. sa S S S ga S S S re ga S S S pa ma S S S ga ma re S S ga S S S pa S S S dha S S S S ^{dha}ni S S S S ^{sa}ni S S S sa S S S
   S ga S S S S ma re S S S sa S S S S re sa ni S S S S sa ni dha pa S S S dha S S S ^{dha}ni S S dha S S S pa S S ma ga
   ma S S S re S S S sa S S S S

5. sa S S S S ni dha S S S sa S S S ga S S S regapadhani dha S S S pa dha ni dha pa ma ga ma re S S S sa S S S S

RAAG ALHAIYA BILAWAL   (Teen Taal)

sthayi: Kirapaa karo sri Seeta Raama ava
             Dha puree ke Raama mope

antara: Aayaa hun main sharana tihaaree
             Kirapaa karo mere Raama mope

sthayi:

maga	ni	dha	pa	maga	rega	pa	ma	ga	ma	re	sani	re	sa,	ga	re
kira	paa	s	ka	ro s	ss	sri	s	see	s	taa	ss	raa	ma	a	va
0				3				x				2			

ga	pa	pa	pa	dha	ni	sa	re	sare	sani	dhapa	dhani	dhapa	ma	ga,	maga
dha	pu	ree	s	ke	s	raa	s	ss	ss	ss	ss	ss	s	ma	mope
0				3				x				2			

antara:

ga	pa	dha	ni	sa	sa	sa	-	sa	gare	ga	ma	gare	sa	sani	sa
aa	s	yaa	s	hun	s	main s		sha	ra s	na	ti	haa s	s	ree s	s
0				3				x				2			

sani	re	sa	ni	dha	pa	ma	ga	gapa	dhani	sani	dhapa	dhani	dhapa	ma	ga
ki s	ra	paa	ka	ro	s	me	re	raa s	ss	ss	ss	ss	s ma	mo	pe
0				3				x				2			

अल्हैया बिलावल

थाठ बिलावल स्वर-सा रे ग म प ध नि

स्वर-इस राग में सभी शुद्ध स्वरों का प्रयोग होता है। अवरोह करते समय धैवत के साथ निषाद कोमल का प्रयोग होता है। जैसे- सां नि ध प, ध नि ध प,

जाति-षाढव/सम्पूर्ण   ६/७

वादी-धैवत

सम्वादी-गंधार

गायन समय-दिन का प्रथम प्रहर

पकड़- ग रे ग प म ग म रे ग प ध नि सा नि ध प ध नि प

आरोह-सा रे ग प ध नि सां

अवरोह-सां नि ध प ध नि ध प म ग रे सा

आलाप-

१. सा ऽ ऽ ऽ ग़ ऽ ऽ ऽ ग म रे ऽ ऽ ऽ सा ऽ ऽ ऽ ऽ ऽ सा रे सा नि ध ऽ ऽ ऽ नि ऽ ऽ ऽ सां नि सा ऽ ऽ ऽ ऽ ऽ

२. सा ऽ ऽ ऽ ग ऽ ऽ ऽ रे ग ऽ ऽ ऽ ऽ प ऽ ऽ ऽ म ऽ ऽ ग ऽ ऽ ऽ ग म ऽ ऽ ऽ रे ऽ ऽ सा रे ग ऽ ऽ ऽ ऽ प ऽ ऽ ऽ ध ऽ ऽ ऽ नि ध प ऽ ऽ ग प म ऽ ऽ ऽ ग म रे ऽ ऽ ऽ ग प ऽ ऽ ऽ ऽ ध नि ऽ ऽ ऽ ध प ऽ ऽ ऽ ऽ म ऽ ऽ ऽ ग म रे ऽ ऽ ऽ सा ऽ ऽ ऽ ऽ

३. सा रे ऽ ऽ ग ऽ ऽ ऽ ग प ऽ ऽ ऽ ध ऽ ऽ ऽ नि ऽ ऽ ऽ सां ऽ ऽ ऽ ऽ सारें सां नि ध ऽ ऽ ऽ प ऽ ऽ ऽ ध नि ध ऽ ऽ ऽ प ऽ ऽ ऽ म ग म रे ऽ ग प ऽ ऽ म ग ऽ ऽ ऽ ऽ म रे ऽ ऽ सा ऽ ऽ

४. सा ऽ ऽ ऽ ग ऽ ऽ ऽ रे ग ऽ ऽ ऽ प म ऽ ऽ ऽ ग म रे ऽ ऽ ग ऽ ऽ ऽ प ऽ ऽ ऽ ध ऽ ऽ ऽ ध़ नि ऽ ऽ ऽ ऽ सां नि ऽ ऽ ऽ सां ऽ ऽ ऽ ऽ गं ऽ ऽ ऽ ऽ मं रें ऽ ऽ ऽ सां ऽ ऽ ऽ ऽ रें सां नि ऽ ऽ ऽ सां नि ध प ऽ ऽ ऽ ध ऽ ऽ ऽ ध़ नि ऽ ऽ ध ऽ ऽ ऽ प ऽ ऽ ऽ म ग म ऽ ऽ ऽ ऽ रे ऽ ऽ सा ऽ ऽ ऽ

५. सा ऽ ऽ ऽ ऽ नि ध़ ऽ ऽ ऽ सा ऽ ऽ ऽ ग ऽ ऽ ऽ रे ग प ध नि ध ऽ ऽ ऽ प ध नि ध प म ग म रे ऽ ऽ ऽ सा ऽ ऽ ऽ ऽ ऽ

राग अल्हैया बिलावल (त्रिताल)

स्थाई- किरपा करो श्री सीता राम अव
धपुरी के राम मोपे

अन्तरा- आया हूँ मैं शरन तिहारी
किरपा करो मेरे राम मोपे

स्थाई-

मुग	नि	ध	प	मुग	रेग	प	म	ग	म	रे	सानि	रे	सा,	ग	रे
किर	पा	ऽ	क	रोऽ	ऽऽ	श्री	ऽ	सी	ऽ	ता	ऽऽ	रा	म	अव	
०				३				x				२			

ग	प	प	प	ध	नि	सां	रें	सांरें	सानिं	धप	धनि	धप	मुग	म	ग
ध	पु	री	ऽ	के	ऽ	रा	ऽ	ऽऽ	ऽऽ	ऽऽ	ऽऽ	ऽऽ	ऽम	मो	पे
०				३				x				२			

अन्तरा-

ग	प	ध	नि	सां	सां	सां	-	सां	गरें	गं	मं	गरें	सां	सानि	सां
आ	ऽ	या	ऽ	हूँ	ऽ	मैं	ऽ	श	रऽ	न	ति	हाऽ	ऽ	रीऽ	ऽ
०				३				x				२			

सानि	रें	सां	नि	ध	प	म	ग	गप	धनि	सानि	धप	धनि	धप	म	ग
किऽ	र	प	क	रोऽ	ऽ	मे	रे	राऽ	ऽऽ	ऽऽ	ऽऽ	ऽऽ	ऽम	मो	पे
०				३				x				२			

RAAG KHAMAJ

thaat khamaj: sa re ga ma pa dha ni

swara: In this raag both shuddh and komal ni are used; all the rest are shuddh swaras. However, during the aroh, re is not used. Komal ni is not used in the aroh but is used in the avaroh.

jati: shadhav/sampurn   6/7

vadi swara: ga

samvadi swara: ni

time of singing: second prahara (second part of the night)

pakar: ni dha, ma pa dha, ma ga

aroh: sa ga ma pa dha ni sà

avaroh: sà ni dha pa ma ga re sa

alaap:

1. sa S S S ga S S S re S S sa S S S saresani dha ma pa dha ni S S S ˢᵃni sa S S S S

2. sa ga S S S sa ga ma pa dha S S S S ma pa dha S S S ma ga S S S S pa ma ga re S S S sa ga S S S S ma ga re sa S S S S S

3. ga ma pa dha S S S ma pa dha S S S ni dha ma pa dha S S S S ma ga S S S gamapadha ni dha ni dha, ma pa dha S S S ni S S S sà S S S S

4. re sà ni dha S S S ma pa dha S S S ma ga S S S S sa ga ma pa, ga ma pa S S S ga ma pa dha ni dha S S S ma dha S S S ma ga S S S re sa S

5. sa ga ma pa dha, ma pa dha S S S ga ma pa ni dha ni dha pa dha ni sà ni sà ni dha S S S ma pa dha ma ga S S S re sa

RAAG KHAMAJ (Ek Taal)

sthayi:
Sohata gala munda maala
Vairaagee vesha dhare
Teena loka tribhuvanapatee
Jataa ganga triputa bhaala

antara:
Rudra roopa traya netra bhaala
Kailaashapati deenana pratipaala
Dhyaavat rishi muni baara baara
Gale vishadhara daale maala

sthayi:

sa	sa	ga	ga	ga	ma	pa	dha	ga	pama	gare	ga
So	ꕯ	ha	ta	ga	la	mu	ꕯ	nda	maaꕯ	ꕯꕯ	la
x		0		2		0		3		4	

ga	ma	pa	-	padha	sa	ni	dha	pa	ma	ga	ma
Vai	ꕯ	ra	ꕯ	geeꕯ	ꕯ	ve	ꕯ	sha	dha	re	ꕯ
x		0		2		0		3		4	

ma	ni	dha	ni	pa	dha	ni	sa	ni	sa	sa	sa
tee	ꕯ	na	lo	ꕯ	ka	tri	bhu	va	na	pa	ti
x		0		2		0		3		4	

pani	sare	sani	sa	ni	dhapa	ma	pa	dha	pa	ma	ga
Jaꕯ	taaꕯ	ꕯꕯ	gan	ꕯ	gaꕯ	tri	pu	ta	maa	ꕯ	la
x		0		2		0		3		4	

antara:

ma	ni	dha	ni	pa	dha	ni	sa	ni	sa	sa	sa
Ru	S	dra	roo	S	pa	tra	ya	ne	tra	bhaa	la
x		0		2		0		3		4	

ni	ni	sa	sa	sa	re	dha	sa	ni	dha	pa	dha
Kai	laa	sha	pa	ti	dee	na	na	pra	ti	paa	la
x		0		2		0		3		4	

ga	ni	dha	ni	pa	dha	ni	sa	ni	sa	sa	sa
Dhya	S	vat	S	ri	shi	mu	ni	baa	ra	baa	ra
x		0		2		0		3		4	

pani	sare	sani	sa	ni	dhapa	dha	ma	pa	dha	ma	ga
Ga S	le S	vi S	sha	dha	ra S	daa	S	le	maa	S	la
x		0		2		0		3		4	

राग खमाज

थाठ खमाज- सा रे ग म प ध नि

स्वर- इस राग में दोनों निशाद बाकी शुद्ध स्वरों का प्रयोग होता है। आरोह में कोमल निशाद वर्जित।

जाति- षाढव/सम्पूर्ण   ६/७

वादी- गंधार

सम्वादी- निशाद

गायन समय- रात्रि द्वितीय प्रहर

पकड़- नि॒ ध, म प ध, म ग

आरोह- सा ग म प ध नि सां

अवरोह- सां नि॒ ध प म ग रे सा

आलाप-

१. सा ऽ ऽ ऽ ग ऽ ऽ ऽ रे ऽ ऽ सा ऽ ऽ ऽ सा रे सा नि॒ ध म॒ प॒ ध नि॒ ऽ ऽ ऽ सांनि॒ सा ऽ ऽ ऽ ऽ

२. सा ग ऽ ऽ ऽ सा ग म प ध ऽ ऽ ऽ ऽ म प ध ऽ ऽ ऽ ऽ म ग ऽ ऽ ऽ ऽ प म ग रे ऽ ऽ ऽ सा ग ऽ ऽ ऽ ऽ म ग रे सा ऽ ऽ ऽ ऽ

३. ग म प ध ऽ ऽ ऽ म प ध ऽ ऽ ऽ ऽ नि॒ ध म प ध ऽ ऽ ऽ ऽ म ग ऽ ऽ ऽ ग म प ध नि॒ ध नि॒ ध, म प ध ऽ ऽ ऽ नि ऽ ऽ ऽ सां ऽ ऽ ऽ ऽ

४. रें सां नि॒ ध ऽ ऽ ऽ म प ध ऽ ऽ ऽ म ग ऽ ऽ ऽ ऽ सा ग म प, ग म प ऽ ऽ ऽ ग म प ध नि॒ ध ऽ ऽ ऽ म ध ऽ ऽ ऽ म ग ऽ ऽ ऽ रे सा ऽ

५. सा ग म प ध, म प ध ऽ ऽ ऽ ग म प नि॒ ध नि॒ ध प ध नि सां नि सां नि॒ ध ऽ ऽ ऽ म प ध म ग ऽ ऽ रे सा

राग खमाज   (एक ताल)

स्थाई- सोहत गल मुण्ड माल
वैरागी वेष धरे,
तीन लोक त्रिभुवनपती
जटा गंग त्रिपुट भाल

अन्तरा- रुद्र रूप त्रय नेत्र भाल
कैलाश पति दीनन प्रतिपाल
ध्यावत ऋषि मुनि बार बार
गले विष धर डाले माल

स्थाई-

सा	सा	ग	ग	ग	म	प	ध	ग	पुम	गुरे	ग
सो	ऽ	ह	त	ग	ल	मु	ऽ	ण्ड	माऽ	ऽऽ	ल
x		०		२		०		३		४	

ग	म	प	-	पुध	सां	नि	ध	प	म	ग	म
वे	ऽ	रा	ऽ	गीऽ	ऽ	वे	ऽ	ष	ध	रे	ऽ
x		०		२		०		३		४	

म	नि	ध	नि	प	ध	नि	सां	नि	सां	सां	सां
ती	ऽ	न	लो	ऽ	क	त्रि	भु	व	न	प	ति
x		०		२		०		३		४	

पनि	सांरें	सांनि	सां	नि	धप	म	प	ध	प	म	ग
जऽ	टाऽ	ऽऽ	गं	ऽ	गाऽ	त्रि	पु	ट	मा	ऽ	ल
x		०		२		०		३		४	

अन्तरा-

म	नि	ध	नि	प	ध	नि	सां	नि	सां	सां	सां
रू	s	द्र	रू	s	प	त्र	य	ने	त्र	भा	ल
x		०		२		०		३		४	

नि	नि	सां	सां	सां	रें	ध	सां	नि	ध	प	ध
कै	ला	श	प	ति	दी	न	न	प्र	ति	पा	ल
x		०		२		०		३		४	

ग	नि	ध	नि	प	ध	नि	सां	नि	सां	सां	सां
ध्या	s	व	त	ऋ	षि	मु	नि	बा	र	बा	र
x		०		२		०		३		४	

पनि	सारें	संनि	सां	नि	धप	ध	म	प	ध	म	ग
गऽ	लेऽ	विऽ	ष	ध	रऽ	डा	s	ले	मा	s	ल
x		०		२		०		३		४	

RAAG KAFI

thaat kafi: sa re ga ma pa dha ni
swara: In this raag both ga and ni are komal, the other five swaras are shuddh. Thus this raag consists of all seven swaras.
jati: sampurn/sampurn   7/7
vadi swara: pa
samvadi swara: sa
time of singing: midnight
pakar: sa sa re re ga ga ma ma pa
aroh: sa re ga ma pa dha ni sa
avaroh: sa ni dha pa ma ga re sa

alaap:

1. sa re ga ꜱ ꜱ ꜱ re sa ꜱ ꜱ ꜱ ni sa ga ꜱ ꜱ re ma ꜱ ꜱ ꜱ ga re ꜱ ꜱ ꜱ ꜱ sa ꜱ ꜱ ꜱ

2. sa re ga ꜱ ꜱ ma ꜱ ꜱ ꜱ pa ꜱ ꜱ ꜱ ga ꜱ ꜱ ꜱ re ꜱ ꜱ ma ꜱ ꜱ ꜱ pa ꜱ ꜱ ꜱ ga re ꜱ ꜱ ꜱ ga sa re ni ꜱ ꜱ ꜱ ꜱ sa ꜱ ꜱ ꜱ

3. sa re ga ꜱ ꜱ ma ꜱ ꜱ pa dha ni dha pa ꜱ ꜱ ꜱ ꜱ ma pa ga re ꜱ ꜱ ꜱ ma ꜱ ꜱ pa ꜱ ꜱ ꜱ dha ꜱ ꜱ ꜱ ni dha pa ꜱ ꜱ ꜱ ma pa dha ni ꜱ ꜱ
sa ꜱ ꜱ ꜱ sa ni dha pa ma ga ꜱ ꜱ re ga ꜱ ꜱ sa re ma pa ga re ꜱ sa ꜱ ꜱ ꜱ

4. ma pa dha ni dha pa ga re ꜱ ꜱ ma ꜱ ꜱ pa ꜱ ꜱ dha ꜱ ꜱ ni ꜱ ꜱ sa ꜱ ꜱ ꜱ re ꜱ ꜱ ꜱ ga ꜱ ꜱ re sa ꜱ ꜱ ꜱ ꜱ ni dha pa ꜱ ꜱ ꜱ ꜱ ga re ꜱ ꜱ ꜱ
ma pa ꜱ ꜱ ꜱ ga re ꜱ ꜱ sa ꜱ ꜱ ꜱ

RAAG KAFI   (Teen Taal)

sthayi: Khelana chalo ali ri kujana holee
Khelana chalo aali ree bajata dhapha
Mrdanga dheere dheere nagi nata kira taka
Naka dhuma kita taka dhaa kita taki ta na kaa dhi ttaa
Tita kata gada gina dhaa holee

antara: Jhorina abeera kara kamalana pichakaaree
Gaavata bajaavata hasata saba dai dai taalee
Nanda dulaaraa Raama daas ka prana piyaaraa bansee vaalaa
Dhooma machaave chaachara gaave vo kaali ree holee

sthayi:

sa	re	re	ga	ma	ma	pa	ma	pa	-	-	ma	ga	re	sa	ni̱
khe	la	na	cha	lo	aa	ꜱ	li	ree	ꜱ	ꜱ	ku	ja	na,	ho	lee
0				3				x				2			

sa	re	re	ga	ma	ma	pa	ma	pa	-	-	ma	pa	dha	ni̱	sȧ
khe	la	na	cha	lo	aa	ꜱ	li	ree	ꜱ	ꜱ	ba	ja	ta	dha	pha
0				3				x				2			

ma	dha	-	pa	ga	ga	re	re	gani	nini	nini	nini	dhadha	dhadha	papa	papa
mr	dan	ꜱ	ga	dhee	re	dhee	re	nagi	nata	kira	taka	naka	dhuma	kita	taka
0				3				x				2			

ma	mama	papa	padha	pa	-	pa	dha	papa	papa	mama	gaga	re	-,	sa	ni̱
dhaa	kita	taki	tana	kaa	ꜱ	dhi	ttaa	tita	kata	gada	gina	dhaa	ꜱ,	ho	lee
0				3				x				2			

INDIAN MUSIC

antara:

ma	ma	ma	ma	pa	pa	ni	ni	sa	sa	sa	sa	re	ni	sa	sa
Jho	ri	na	a	bee	ra	ka	ra	ka	ma	la	na	pi	cha	kaa	ree
0				3				x				2			

ni	ni	ni	ni	dha	dha	pa	pa	ma	ma	pa	pa	ga	ga	re	re
gaa	va	ta	ba	jaa	va	ta	he	sa	ta	sa	ba	dai	dai	taa	lee
0				3				x				2			

rere	ni	ni	ni	dha	dhadha	dha	pa	mama	ma	pa	pa	ga	ga	re	sa
nanS	da	du	laa	raa	raama	daas kaa		praana	pi	yaa	ra	ban	see	vaa	laa
0				3				x				2			

sasa	sa	sa	sa	ni	nini	dha	pa	pa		pa	dha	pa	ga	re	sa	ni
dhooma	ma	chaa	ve	chaa	chara	gaa	ve	vo	kaa	S	li	ree	S,	ho	lee	
0				3				x				2				

60

राग काफी

थाठ काफी-सा रे ग॒ म प ध नि॒
स्वर-इस राग में ग॒, कोमल तथा दोनों नि, का प्रयोग होता है। आरोह में शुद्ध तथा अवरोह कोमल नि॒।
जाति-सम्पूर्ण/सम्पूर्ण   ७/७
वादी-पंचम
सम्वादी-षड्ज
गाने का समय-मध्य रात्रि
पकड़-सा॒सा रे रे ग॒ ग॒ म म प
आरोह-सा रे ग॒ म प ध नि सां
अवरोह-सां नि॒ ध प म ग॒ रे सा

आलाप-

१. सा रे ग॒ ऽ ऽ ऽ रे सा ऽ ऽ ऽ नि॒ सा ग॒ ऽ ऽ रे म ऽ ऽ ऽ ग॒ रे ऽ ऽ ऽ ऽ सा ऽ ऽ ऽ ऽ

२. सा रे ग॒ ऽ ऽ म ऽ ऽ ऽ प ऽ ऽ ऽ ग॒ ऽ ऽ ऽ रे ऽ ऽ म ऽ ऽ ऽ प ऽ ऽ ऽ ग॒ रे ऽ ऽ ऽ ग॒ सा रे नि॒ ऽ ऽ ऽ सा ऽ ऽ ऽ

३. सा रे ग॒ ऽ म ऽ ऽ प ध नि॒ ध प ऽ ऽ ऽ म प ग॒ रे ऽ ऽ ऽ म ऽ ऽ प ऽ ऽ ऽ ध ऽ ऽ ऽ नि॒ ध प ऽ ऽ ऽ म प ध नी ऽ ऽ सां ऽ ऽ
ऽ सां नि॒ ध प म ग॒ ऽ ऽ रे ग॒ ऽ ऽ सा रे म प ग॒ रे सा ऽ ऽ ऽ

४. म प ध नि॒ ध प ग॒ रे ऽ ऽ म ऽ ऽ प ऽ ऽ ध ऽ ऽ नि॒ ऽ ऽ सां ऽ ऽ ऽ रें॒ ऽ ऽ गं॒ ऽ ऽ रें सां ऽ ऽ ऽ ऽ नि॒ ध प ऽ ऽ ऽ ऽ ग॒ रे ऽ ऽ ऽ म
प ऽ ऽ ऽ ग॒ रे ऽ ऽ सा ऽ ऽ ऽ

61

राग काफी   (तीन ताल)

स्थाई- खेलन चलो आलिरी कुजन, होली

खेलन चलो आलिरी बजत दफ

मृदंग धीरे धीरे नगि नन किर तक तक धूम किट तक

धा कट तकि टन का धित्ता तिट कत गद गिन धा, होली

अन्तरा- झोरिन अबीर कर कमलन पिचकारी

गावत बजावत हसत सब दै दै ताली

नन्द दुलारा राम दास का प्राण पियारा बन्सीवाला

धूम मचावे चाचर गावे बोकालिरी, होली

स्थाई-

सा	रे	रे	<u>ग</u>	म	म	प	म	प	–	–	म	<u>ग</u>	रे,	सा	नि
खे	ल	न	च	लो	आ	ऽ	लि	री	ऽ	ऽ	कु	ज	न,	हो	ली
०				३				x				२			

सा	रे	रे	<u>ग</u>	म	म	प	म	प	–	–	म	प	ध	<u>नि</u>	सां
खे	ल	न	च	लो	आ	ऽ	लि	री	ऽ	ऽ	ब	ज	त	ढ	फ
०				३				x				२			

म	ध	–	प	<u>ग</u>	<u>ग</u>	रे	रे	<u>गनि</u>	<u>निनि</u>	<u>निनि</u>	<u>निनि</u>	धध,	धध,	पप,	पप
मृ	दं	ऽ	ग	धी	रे	धी	रे	नगि	नन	किर	तक	तक	धूम	किट	तक
०				३				x				२			

म	<u>मम</u>	<u>पप</u>	<u>पध</u>	प	–	प	ध	<u>पप</u>	<u>पप</u>	<u>मम</u>	<u>गग</u>	रे	–,	सा	नि
धा	किट	तकि	टन	का	ऽ	धि	त्ता	तिट	कत	गद	गिन	धा	ऽ,	हो	ली
०				३				x				२			

अन्तरा-

म	म	म	म	प	प	नि	नि	सां	सां	सां	सां	रें	नि	सां	सां
झो	रि	न	अ	बी	र	क	र	क	म	ल	न	पि	च	का	री
०				३				x				२			

नि	नि	नि	नि	ध	ध	प	प	म	म	प	प	ग	ग	रे	रे
गा	व	त	ब	जा	व	त	ह	स	त	स	ब	दै	दै	ता	ली
०				३				x				२			

रेरे	नि	नि	नि	ध	धध	ध	प	मुम	म	प	प	ग	ग	रे	सां
नन्द	दु	ला	रा	रा	मदा	स	का	प्राण	पि	या	रा	ब	न्सी	वा	ल
०				३				x				२			

सासा	सां	सां	सां	नि	निनि	ध	प	प	प	ध	प	ग	रे,	सा	नि
धुम	म	चा	वे	चा	चर	गा	वे	वो	का	ऽ	लि	री	ऽ,	हो	ली
०				३				x				२			

RAAG BHAIRAV   (Teen Taal)

thaat bhairava: sa re ga ma pa dha ni
swara: This raag consists of all seven swaras. Re and dha are komal, the rest are shuddh.
jati: sampurn/sampurn   7/7
vadi swara: dha
samvadi swara: re
time of singing: morning
pakar: ga ma dha S S S pa ga ma re S S S sa S S S
aroh: sa re ga ma pa dha ni sa
avaroh: sa ni dha pa ma ga re sa

alaap:

1. sa re S S re S S S sa S S ˢᵃdha S S S ni S S sa S S saresani dha S S S pa S S S dha S S dha S S S ni sa S S

2. sa re S re S sa S S ga ma re S re S sa S S S sa re ga ma, gamapama dha S S dha S S S pa S S

3. sa ga ma pa, dha S S S dha S S S pa ma pa S S S S ga ma dha S S S S S pa S S S S ma pa dha S S S ni S
   S sa S S S S ˢᵃdha S S ni sa S S re S S S re S S S sa S S S S S

4. sa S S re S S re S S S sa ni dha S S S ni S S sa re S S re S S S sa S S S S

5. ga ma S S S S ga ma re S S S S sa S S S ma S S S S ma pa S S S dha S S S dha S S S pa S S S S gamapama
   ga re S S S re S S S sa S S S S

RAAG BHAIRAV   (Teen Taal)

sthayi: Bhora bhaee jaago nandalaala
Dvaara khare saba gvaala baala

antara: Gauven charaao muralee bajaao
Maata yashodaa ke pyaare laal

sthayi:

sa	dha	pa	pa	ma	-	ma	-	ga	-	gama	pama	re	-	sa	sa
bho	ꜱ	ra	bha	ee	ꜱ	jaa	ꜱ	go	ꜱ	nanꜱ	daꜱ	laa	ꜱ	ꜱ	la
3				x				2				0			

ma	-	pa	pa	sà	-	dha	dha	gama	pama	ma	ga	re	sa	-	-
dvaa	ꜱ	ra	kha	re	ꜱ	sa	ba	gvaaꜱ	ꜱꜱ	la	baa	ꜱ	la	ꜱ	ꜱ
3				x				2				0			

antara:

ma	ma	pa	dha	dhani	sà	sà	-	rè	-	rè	rè	ṣani	dhani	sà	-
ga	u	ven	cha	raaꜱ	o	ꜱ	mu	ra	lee	ba	jaa	ꜱꜱ	ꜱo	ꜱ	ꜱ
3				x				2				0			

sà	dha	pa	ma	dha	-	pa	pa	gama	pama	ga	rega	mapa	maga	resa	sa
maa	ꜱ	ta	ya	sho	ꜱ	daa	ke	pyaaꜱ	ꜱꜱ	re	laaꜱ	ꜱꜱ	ꜱꜱ	ꜱꜱ	l
3				x				2				0			

राग भैरव

थाठ भैरव-सा रे॒ ग म प ध॒ नि

स्वर- इस राग में रे॒, ध॒, कोमल बाकी के शुद्ध स्वरों का प्रयोग होता है।

जाति-सम्पूर्ण/सम्पूर्ण ७/७

वादी- धैवत

सम्वादी- रिषव

गाने का समय- प्रातःकाल

पकड़- ग म ध॒ऽऽऽ प ग म रे॒ऽऽऽ साऽऽऽ

आरोह- सा रे॒ ग म प ध॒ नि सां

अवरोह- सां नि ध॒ प म ग रे॒ सा

आलाप-

१. सा रे॒ ऽ ऽ रे॒ ऽ ऽ ऽ सा ऽ ऽ सां ध॒ ऽ ऽ ऽ नि ऽ ऽ सा ऽ ऽ सां रे॒ सां नि ध॒ ऽ ऽ ऽ प ऽ ऽ ऽ ध॒ ऽ ऽ ध॒ ऽ ऽ नि॒ सा ऽ ऽ

२. सा रे॒ ऽ रे॒ ऽ सा ऽ ऽ ग म रे॒ ऽ रे॒ ऽ सा ऽ ऽ ऽ सा रे॒ ग म, गमपम ध॒ ऽ ऽ ध॒ ऽ ऽ ऽ प ऽ ऽ

३. सा ग म प, ध॒ ऽ ऽ ऽ ध॒ ऽ ऽ ऽ प म प ऽ ऽ ऽ ऽ ग म ध॒ ऽ ऽ ऽ ऽ ऽ ऽ प ऽ ऽ ऽ ऽ म प ध॒ ऽ ऽ ऽ ऽ नि ऽ ऽ सां ऽ ऽ ऽ ऽ सांध॒ ऽ
नि सां ऽ ऽ रें॒ ऽ ऽ ऽ रें॒ ऽ ऽ ऽ सां ऽ ऽ ऽ ऽ

४. सा ऽ ऽ रे॒ ऽ ऽ रे॒ ऽ ऽ ऽ सा नि॒ ध॒ ऽ ऽ ऽ नि॒ ऽ ऽ सा रे॒ ऽ ऽ रे॒ ऽ ऽ ऽ सा ऽ ऽ ऽ ऽ

५. ग म ऽ ऽ ऽ ऽ ग म रे॒ ऽ ऽ ऽ ऽ सा ऽ ऽ ऽ म ऽ ऽ ऽ ऽ म प ऽ ऽ ध॒ ऽ ऽ ऽ ध॒ ऽ ऽ ऽ प ऽ ऽ ऽ ऽ गमपम ग रे॒ ऽ ऽ रे॒ ऽ ऽ ऽ
सा ऽ ऽ ऽ ऽ

राग भैरव   (तीन ताल)

स्थाई-   भोर भई जागो नन्द लाल
द्वार खड़े सब ग्वाल बाल

अन्तरा-   गउवें चराओ मुरली बजाओ
मात यशोदा के प्यारे लाल

स्थाई-

सा	ध	प	प	म	-	म	-	ग	-	गम	पम	रे	-	सा	सा
भो	ऽ	र	भ	इ	ऽ	जा	ऽ	गो	ऽ	नऽ	न्दऽ	ला	ऽ	ऽ	ल
३				x				२				०			

म	-	प	प	सां	-	ध	ध	गम	पम	म	ग	रे	सा	-	-
द्वा	ऽ	र	ख	ड़े	ऽ	स	ब	ग्वा	ऽऽ	ल	बा	ऽ	ल	ऽ	ऽ
३				x				२				०			

अन्तरा-

म	म	प	ध	धनि	सां	सां	-	रे	-	रे	रे	सांनि	धनिं	सां	-
ग	उ	वें	च	राऽ	ओ	ऽ	मु	र	ली	ब	जा	ऽऽ	ऽओ	ऽ	ऽ
३				x				२				०			

सां	ध	प	म	ध	-	प	प	गम	पम	ग	रेग	मप	मग	रेसा	सा
मा	ऽ	त	य	शो	ऽ	दा	के	प्याऽ	ऽऽ	रे	लाऽ	ऽऽ	ऽऽ	ऽऽ	ल
३				x				२				०			

RAAG ASAVARI

thaat asavari: sa re ga ma pa dha ni

swara: In this raag, ga, dha, and ni are komal, the other five swaras are shuddh. During the aroh ga and ni are not used.

jati: audav/sampurn   5/7

vadi swara: dha

samvadi swara: ga

time of singing: second part of the day

pakar: ma pa dha, pa dha ma pa ga, re sa

aroh: sa re ma pa dha sa

avaroh: sa ni dha pa, ma pa ma ga re sa

alaap:

1. sa re sa S S S ˢᵃdha S S sa S S S re S S sa sa re ma pa ga S S S S re S S sa S S S ni dha S S S pa S S S ma pa dha S S S sa S S S S S

2. sa re ma S S pa S S S ma pa dha ma S S S pa S S S S ga S S S re S S S sa S S S re ma pa S S S dha S S dha S pa S S ma pa ni dha S S S pa S S S padhamapa ga S S S S re sa S S S S

3. sa re ma pa ni dha S S S pa S S ma pa dha S S S S sa ni dha S S pa S S ma pa ni dha S S S pa pa dha ma pa ga S S S re S S sa

4. sa re ma pa dha S S dha S S S pa S S S ma pa ni dha S S S pa S S ma pa dha sa S S S re ni dha S S S pa S S ma pa dha S dha sa S S S S ni dha pa S S ma pa ni S dha S pa S S ga S S re S S sa S S

5. sa re ma pa ni dha S S pa S S S dha S S S sa S S S S reresani dha S S S pa S S S mapaninidhapa S S pa dha ma pa ga S S S re S S sa S S S

68

RAAG ASAVARI   (Teen Taal)

sthayi: Tuma bina kauna kripaalu deenana para,
deena vandhu dukha haaree

antara: Adhama udhaarana patita paavana
karanaakara tripuraaree

sthayi:

dha	ma	pa	sa	dha	pa	pa	pa	dha	ma	padha	mapa	ga	ga	re	sa
tu	ma	bi	na	kau	ꜱ	na	kri	paa	ꜱ	luꜱ	deeꜱ	na	na	pa	ra
3				x				2				0			

re	ma	re	ma	pa	ma	pa	dha	sare	gare	sani	dhapa	mapa	dhapa	maga	resa
di	ꜱ	na	ba	ꜱ	ndhu	du	kha	haaꜱ	ꜱꜱ	ꜱꜱ	ꜱꜱ	ꜱꜱ	ꜱꜱ	ꜱꜱ	reeꜱ
3				x				2				0			

antara:

ma	ma	ma	ma	pa	-	dha	dha	sa	sa	sa	sa	re	ni	sa	sa
a	dha	ma	u	dha	ꜱ	ra	na	pa	ti	ta	ꜱ	paa	ꜱ	va	na
3				x				2				0			

dha	dha	ga	ga	re	re	sa	sa	nisa	rere	sani	dhapa	mapa	dhapa	maga	resa
ka	ru	naa	ꜱ	ka	ra	tri	pu	raaꜱ	ꜱꜱ	ꜱꜱ	ꜱꜱ	ꜱꜱ	ꜱꜱ	ꜱꜱ	reeꜱ
3				x				2				0			

69

राग आसावरी

थाठ आसावरी- सा रे <u>ग</u> म प <u>ध</u> <u>नि</u>

स्वर- इस राग में गंधार, धैवत, निशाद स्वर कोमल लगते हैं। बाकी के शुद्ध स्वरों का प्रयोग होता है। आरोह करते समय गंधार निशाद स्वर वर्जित है।

जाति- ओढव/सम्पूर्ण   ५/७

वादी- धैवत

सम्वादी- गंधार

गाने का समय- दिन का दूसरा प्रहर

पकड़- म प <u>ध</u>, प <u>ध</u> म प <u>ग</u>, रे सा

आरोह- सा रे म प <u>ध</u> सां

अवरोह- सां <u>नि</u> <u>ध</u> प, म प म <u>ग</u>, रे सा

आलाप-

१. सा रे सा ऽऽऽ^{सा}<u>ध</u> ऽऽ सा ऽऽऽ रें ऽऽ सा सा रे म प <u>ग</u> ऽऽऽऽ रें ऽऽ सा ऽऽऽ <u>नि</u> <u>ध</u> ऽऽऽ प ऽऽऽ म प <u>ध</u> ऽऽऽ सा ऽऽऽऽऽ

२. सा रे म ऽऽ प ऽऽऽ म प <u>ध</u> म ऽऽऽ प ऽऽऽऽ <u>ग</u> ऽऽऽ रें ऽऽ सा ऽऽऽ रे म प ऽऽऽ <u>ध</u> ऽऽ <u>ध</u> प ऽऽ म प <u>नि</u> <u>ध</u> ऽऽऽ प ऽऽ प <u>ध</u>मप <u>ग</u> ऽऽऽ रे सा ऽऽऽऽ

३. सा रे म प <u>नि</u> <u>ध</u> ऽऽऽ प ऽऽ म प <u>ध</u> ऽऽऽऽ सां <u>नि</u> <u>ध</u> ऽऽ प ऽऽ म प <u>नि</u> <u>ध</u> ऽऽऽ प प <u>ध</u> म प <u>ग</u> ऽऽऽ रें ऽऽ सा

४. सा रे म प <u>ध</u> ऽऽ <u>ध</u> ऽऽऽ प ऽऽऽ म प <u>नि</u> <u>ध</u> ऽऽऽ प ऽऽ म प <u>ध</u> सां ऽऽऽ रें <u>नि</u> <u>ध</u> ऽऽऽ प ऽऽ म प <u>ध</u> <u>ध</u> सां ऽ ऽऽऽ <u>नि</u> <u>ध</u> प ऽऽ म प <u>नि</u> <u>ध</u> ऽ प ऽऽ <u>ग</u> ऽऽ रे सा ऽऽ

५. सा रे म प <u>नि</u> <u>ध</u> ऽऽ प ऽऽऽ <u>ध</u> ऽऽऽ सां ऽऽऽ रें<u>नि</u>सा<u>नि</u> <u>ध</u> ऽऽऽ प ऽऽऽ म प <u>नि</u><u>नि</u><u>ध</u>प ऽऽ प <u>ध</u> म प <u>ग</u> ऽऽ रे ऽऽ सा ऽऽऽ

राग आसावरी   (तीन ताल)

स्थाई-   तुम बिन कौन कृपालु दीनन पर
दीन बन्धु दुरख हारी

अन्तरा-   अधम उधारन पतित पावन
करुणाकर त्रिपुरारी

स्थाई-

धॉ	म	प	सां	धॉ	प	प	प	धॉ	म	पधॉ	मप	गॉ	गॉ	रे	सा
तुॉ	म	बि	न	कौ	ऽ	न	कृ	पाऽ	ऽ	लुॉ	दीऽ	न	न	प	र
३				x				२				०			

रे	म	रे	म	प	म	प	धॉ	सारें	गॉरें	सॉनि	धॉप	मप	धॉप	मगॉ	रेसा
दीऽ	ऽ	न	ब	ऽ	न्धु	दु	ख	हाऽ	ऽऽ	ऽऽ	ऽऽ	ऽऽ	ऽऽ	ऽऽ	रीऽ
३				x				२				०			

अन्तरा-

म	म	म	म	प	-	धॉ	धॉ	सां	सां	सां	सां	रें	निॉ	सां	सां
अ	ध	म	उ	धा	ऽ	र	न	प	ति	त	ऽ	पा	ऽ	व	न
३				x				२				०			

धॉ	धॉ	गॉ	गॉ	रें	रें	सां	सां	निसां	रेंरें	सॉनि	धॉप	मप	धॉप	मगॉ	रेसा
क	रु	णा	ऽ	क	र	त्रि	पु	राऽ	ऽऽ	ऽऽ	ऽऽ	ऽऽ	ऽऽ	ऽऽ	रीऽ
३				x				२				०			

RAAG BHAIRAVI

thaat: sa re ga ma pa dha ni

swara: In this raag, re, ga, dha, and ni are komal. Nowadays some expert musicians have started using some other swaras as vivadi.

jati: sampurn/sampurn   7/7

vadi swara: ma

samvadi swara: sa

time of singing: morning

pakar: dha ni sa re ga, ma ga re ga sa re sa

aroh: sa re ga ma pa dha ni sa

avaroh: sa ni dha pa ma ga re sa

alaap:

1. sa S S S re S S S sa S S S dha ni S S S sa re sa S S dha ni sa re sa S S S S ga S S re S S S sa S S S S

2. sa re ga S S S S ma ga S S S sa re S S sa S S S pa dha pa S S S ga ma S S ga S S S re S S S sa S S S S

3. dha S S S ni sa re ga S S S sa re sa S S S ga ma pa S S S S dha S S S pa S S gamapamagamaga S S S S sa re sa S S S S

4. ma pa dha S S S ni sa S S S S ga S S S re S S S S sa ni sa S S S S ni dha pa S S S ga ma pa ma ga S S S S S sa re sa S S S S S

5. dha ma dha ni sa S S S S S dha ni sa S S ga S S re S S re S S S sa S S S re S S S S sa ni dha pa ma ga re S S S S sa S S S S

RAAG BHAIRAVI   (Tri Taal)

sthayi: Thumaka thumaka paga paaya liyaa
jhanana jhanana baaje kaandha toree

antara: Mora mukuta peetambara sohe
Noopura baaje taa thaiyaa taa thaiyaa

sthayi:

saga	resa	nire	sani	dhasa	nidha	pa	dha	sa	-	-	ni	pa	dha	pa	-
thuˢ	maˢ	kaˢ	thuˢ	maˢ	kaˢ	pa	ga	paa	ˢ	ˢ	ya	li	ˢ	yaa	ˢ
0				3				x				2			

ga	pa	dha	ni	dha	papa	ga	-	mapa	dha	pa	ma	gare	sare	sa	-
jha	na	na	jha	na	naˢ	baa	ˢ	jeˢ	ˢ	kaandha		toˢ	ˢˢ	ree	ˢ
0				3				x				2			

antara:

ga	ma	dha	ni	sa	sa	sa	ni	sare	ga	re	ni	re	-	sa	-
mo	ˢ	ra	mu	ku	ta	pee	ˢ	taaˢ	ˢ	mba	ra	so	ˢ	he	ˢ
0				3				x				2			

ni	-	sa	sa	re	sani	dha	pa	ga	mapa	dha	pama	ga	sa	re	sa
noo	ˢ	pu	ra	baa	ˢˢ	je	ˢ	taa	thaiˢ	ˢ	yaaˢ	taa	thai	ˢ	yaa
0				3				x				2			

राग भैरवी

थाठ-भैरवी-सा रे॒ ग॒ म प ध॒ नि॒ सां

स्वर-इस राग में रे ग ध नि कोमल स्वर लगते हैं। आज कल गुणीजन विवादी रूप में अन्य स्वरों का प्रयोग करने लगे हैं।

जाति-सम्पूर्ण/सम्पूर्ण ७/७

वादी-मध्यम

सम्वादी-षड्ज

गाने का समय-प्रातःकाल

पकड़-ध॒ नि॒ सा रे॒ ग॒, म ग॒ रे॒ ग॒ सा रे॒ सा

आरोह-सा रे॒ ग॒ म प ध॒ नि॒ सां

अवरोह-सां नि॒ ध॒ प म ग॒ रे॒ सा

अलाप-

१. सा ऽ ऽ ऽ रे॒ ऽ ऽ ऽ सा ऽ ऽ ऽ ध॒ नि॒ ऽ ऽ ऽ सा रे॒ सा ऽ ऽ ध॒ नि॒ सा रे॒ सा ऽ ऽ ऽ ऽ ग॒ ऽ ऽ रे॒ ऽ ऽ ऽ सा ऽ ऽ ऽ ऽ

२. सा रे॒ ग॒ ऽ ऽ ऽ ऽ म ग॒ ऽ ऽ ऽ सा रे॒ ऽ ऽ सा ऽ ऽ ऽ प ध॒ प ऽ ऽ ऽ ग॒ म ऽ ऽ ग॒ ऽ ऽ ऽ रे॒ ऽ ऽ ऽ सा ऽ ऽ ऽ ऽ

३. ध॒ ऽ ऽ ऽ नि॒ सा रे॒ ग॒ ऽ ऽ ऽ सा रे॒ सा ऽ ऽ ऽ ऽ ग॒ म प ऽ ऽ ध॒ ऽ ऽ ऽ प ऽ ऽ ग॒मपमग॒मग॒ ऽ ऽ ऽ ऽ सा रे॒ सा ऽ ऽ ऽ ऽ

४. म प ध॒ ऽ ऽ ऽ नि॒ सां ऽ ऽ ऽ ऽ ऽ गं॒ ऽ ऽ ऽ रें॒ ऽ ऽ ऽ ऽ ऽ सां नि॒ सां ऽ ऽ ऽ ऽ नि॒ ध॒ प ऽ ऽ ऽ ग॒ म प म ग॒ ऽ ऽ ऽ ऽ सा रे॒ सा ऽ ऽ ऽ ऽ ऽ

५. ध॒ म ध॒ नि॒ सां ऽ ऽ ऽ ऽ ऽ ध॒ नि॒ सां ऽ ऽ गं॒ ऽ ऽ रें॒ ऽ ऽ रें॒ ऽ ऽ सां ऽ ऽ ऽ रें॒ ऽ ऽ ऽ ऽ सां नि॒ ध॒ प म ग॒ रे॒ ऽ ऽ ऽ ऽ सा ऽ ऽ ऽ ऽ

राग भैरवी (त्रिताल)

स्थाई ठुमक ठुमक पग पायलिया
   झनन झनन बाजे कान्हा तोरी

अन्तरा मोर मुकुट पीताम्बर सोहे
   नूपुर बाजे ता थैइया ता थैइया

स्थाई-

सांगं	रेंसां	निरें	सांनि	धसां	निध	प	ध	सां	–	–	नि	प	ध	प	–
ठु	मड़	कड़	ठु	मड़	कड़	प	ग	पा	ऽ	ऽ	य	लि	ऽ	या	ऽ
०				३				x				२			

ग	प	ध	नि	ध	पप	ग	–	मप	ध	प	म	गरे	सारे	सा	–
झ	न	न	झ	न	नऽ	बा	ऽ	जेऽ	ऽ	का	न्हा	तोऽ	ऽऽ	री	ऽ
०				३				x				२			

अन्तरा-

ग	म	ध	नि	सां	सां	सां	नि	सांरें	गं	रें	नि	रें	–	सां	–
मो	ऽ	र	मु	कु	ट	पी	ऽ	ताऽ	ऽ	म्बर	र	सो	ऽ	हे	ऽ
०				३				x				२			

नि	–	सां	सां	रें	सांनि	ध	प	ग	मप	ध	पम	ग	सा	रे	सा
नू	ऽ	पु	र	बा	ऽऽ	जे	ऽ	ता	थैऽ	ऽ	याऽ	ता	थैऽ	या	ऽ
०				३				x				२			

RAAG YAMAN

thaat kalyan: sa re ga mȧ pa dha ni
swara: In this raag ma is tivra and the other six swaras are shuddh.
jati: sampurn/sampurn   7/7
vadi swara: ga
samvadi swara: ni
time of singing: first part of the night
pakar: ni re ga re, pa re ga re sa
aroh: ṇi re ga mȧ pa dha ni sȧ
avaroh: sȧ ni dha pa mȧ ga re sa

alaap:

1. ṇi re ga ꕔ ꕔ ꕔ re ꕔ ꕔ ꕔ ṇi re ꕔ ꕔ sa ꕔ ꕔ ꕔ ṇi dha ṇi ꕔ ꕔ ꕔ mȧ dha ni re ꕔ ꕔ ꕔ
   sa ꕔ ꕔ ꕔ ꕔ saresani ꕔ ꕔ ꕔ dha ṇi ꕔ ꕔ ꕔ re sa ꕔ ꕔ ꕔ ꕔ

2. ṇi re ga ꕔ ꕔ ꕔ ᵖᵃre ga ꕔ ꕔ ꕔ ṇi re sa ꕔ ꕔ ꕔ ṇi re ga ꕔ ꕔ ꕔ ṇi re ṇi ga re ꕔ ꕔ
   ṇi re ga ꕔ ꕔ ꕔ pa re ga ꕔ ꕔ ꕔ ṇi re sa ꕔ ꕔ ꕔ

3. ṇi re ga ꕔ ꕔ ꕔ pa re ga ꕔ ꕔ ꕔ ṇi re ga ꕔ ꕔ mȧ ga ꕔ ꕔ ꕔ re ga ꕔ ꕔ ꕔ mȧ dha
   pa ꕔ ꕔ ꕔ ꕔ mȧ ga mȧ dha ni ꕔ ꕔ ꕔ ꕔ mȧ ni dha pa ꕔ ꕔ ꕔ ꕔ ᵖᵃre ga ꕔ ꕔ ꕔ ni
   re sa ꕔ ꕔ

4. ṇi re ga mȧ pa re ga ꕔ ꕔ ꕔ ṇi re ga mȧ ᵖᵃmȧ pa ꕔ ꕔ ꕔ mȧ dha ni ꕔ ꕔ ꕔ
   mȧ ga mȧ dha ni ꕔ ꕔ ꕔ re sȧ ꕔ ꕔ ꕔ ni dha ni pa ꕔ ꕔ ꕔ re ga ꕔ ꕔ ꕔ re ꕔ ꕔ
   sa ꕔ ꕔ ꕔ

5. ṇi re ga mȧ pa ꕔ ꕔ ꕔ mȧ ga ꕔ ꕔ ꕔ mȧ dha ni ꕔ ꕔ ꕔ ꕔ mȧ ni dha pa ꕔ ꕔ
   mȧ dha ni ꕔ ꕔ ꕔ sȧni ꕔ ꕔ ꕔ re sȧ ꕔ ꕔ ꕔ ni rė gȧ ꕔ ꕔ ꕔ rė gȧ rė ꕔ ꕔ ꕔ ni rė sȧ
   ni dha ni ꕔ ꕔ ꕔ pa ꕔ ꕔ ꕔ mȧ ga re ꕔ ꕔ ꕔ ṇi re ga re sa ꕔ ꕔ ꕔ ꕔ

RAAG YAMAN   (Dhruva Pada)   (Char Taal)

sthayi: Paara brahma parameshvara
Purushottama paramaananda
Nanda nandana aanandakanda
Yashodaananda shri govinda

antara: Deenaanaatha dukha bhanjana
Pada namaami madhusoodana
Vaasudeva vana maalee
Vrijapati yadu nanda nandana

sthayi:

pa	mã	ga	ga	re	ga	dha	pa	ga	mã	ga	re
paa	ꜱ	ra	bra	ꜱ	hma	pa	ra	me	ꜱ	sva	ra
x		0		2		0		3		4	

ga	mã	pa	–	dha	pamã	ga	mã	gare	ga	re	sa
pu	ru	so	ꜱ	tta	maꜱ	pa	ra	maaꜱ nan		ꜱ	da
x		0		2		0		3		4	

ni	–	dha	ni	sa	sa	sa	ga	re	ga	–	ga
na	ꜱ	nda	na	nda	na	aa	na	nda	ka	ꜱ	nda
x		0		2		0		3		4	

sa	ni	dha	ni	dha	pa	pa	–	mã	ga	re	ga
ya	sho	daa	na	ꜱ	nda	sri	ꜱ	go	vi	ꜱ	nda
x		0		2		0		3		4	

antara:

ga	ma	dha	sȧ	-	sȧ	sȧ	sȧ	sȧni	rė	sȧ	sȧ
dee	naa	ꜱ	naa	ꜱ	tha	du	kha	bhanꜱꜱ		ja	na
x		0		2		0		3		4	

ni	-	dha	ni	sȧ	sȧ	sȧ	rė	sȧ	ni	dha	pa
pa	ꜱ	da	na	maa	mi	ma	dhu	soo	ꜱ	da	na
x		0		2		0		3		4	

sȧ	gȧ	gȧ	mȧ	rė	sȧ	ni	sȧ	dha	-	pa	-
va	ꜱ	su	de	ꜱ	va	va	na	maa	ꜱ	lee	ꜱ
x		0		2		0		3		4	

ga	ma	pa	dha	ni	dha	pa	-	ma	ma	re	ga
vri	ja	pa	ti	ya	du	nan	ꜱ	da	nan	da	na
x		0		2		0		3		4	

राग यमन

थाठ- कल्याण-सा रे ग म॑ प ध नी

स्वर-इस राग में मध्यम तीव्र बाकी के शुद्ध स्वरों का प्रयोग होता है।

जाति-सम्पूर्ण/सम्पूर्ण   ७/७

वादी-गंधार

सम्वादी-निषाद

गाने का समय- रात्रि का प्रथम प्रहर

पकड़-निॖ रे ग रे, प रे ग रे सा

आरोह-निॖ रे ग म॑ प ध नि सां

अवरोह-सां नि ध प म॑ ग रे सा

आलाप-

१. निॖ रे ग ऽ ऽ ऽ रे ऽ ऽ ऽ निॖ रे ऽ ऽ सा ऽ ऽ ऽ निॖ ध्ॖ निॖ ऽ ऽ ऽ म॑ ध्ॖ निॖ रे ऽ ऽ ऽ सा ऽ ऽ
ऽ ऽ सा रे सा निॖ ऽ ऽ ऽ ध्ॖ निॖ ऽ ऽ ऽ रे सा ऽ ऽ ऽ ऽ

२. निॖ रे ग ऽ ऽ ऽ ॑रे ग ऽ ऽ ऽ निॖ रे सा ऽ ऽ ऽ निॖ रे ग ऽ ऽ ऽ निॖ रे निॖ ग रे ऽ ऽ निॖ रे ग
ऽ ऽ ऽ प रे ग ऽ ऽ ऽ निॖ रे सा ऽ ऽ ऽ

३. निॖ रे ग ऽ ऽ ऽ प रे ग ऽ ऽ ऽ निॖ रे ग ऽ ऽ म॑ ग ऽ ऽ ऽ रे ग ऽ ऽ ऽ म॑ ध प ऽ ऽ ऽ ऽ म॑ ग
म॑ ध निॖ ऽ ऽ ऽ म॑ नि ध प ऽ ऽ ऽ ॑रे ग ऽ ऽ ऽ निॖ रे सा ऽ ऽ

४. निॖ रे ग म॑ प रे ग ऽ ऽ ऽ निॖ रे ग म॑ ऽ ऽ ऽ ॑म॑ प ऽ ऽ ऽ म॑ ध निॖ ऽ ऽ ऽ म॑ ग म॑ ध निॖ
ऽ ऽ ऽ रें सां ऽ ऽ ऽ निॖ ध निॖ प ऽ ऽ ऽ रे ग ऽ ऽ ऽ रे ऽ ऽ सा ऽ ऽ ऽ

५. निॖ रे ग म॑ प ऽ ऽ ऽ म॑ ग ऽ ऽ ऽ म॑ ध निॖ ऽ ऽ ऽ ऽ म॑ नि ध प ऽ ऽ म॑ ध निॖ ऽ ऽ ऽ सां॑ नि
ऽ ऽ ऽ रें सां ऽ ऽ ऽ निॖ रें गं ऽ ऽ ऽ रें गं ऽ रें ऽ ऽ ऽ निॖ रें सां निॖ ध निॖ ऽ ऽ ऽ प ऽ ऽ ऽ म॑
ग रे ऽ ऽ ऽ निॖ रे ग रे सा ऽ ऽ ऽ ऽ

राग यमन (धुवपद) (चार ताल)

स्थाई- पार ब्रह्म परमेश्वर
पुरुषोत्तम परमानन्द
नन्द नन्दन आनन्दकन्द
यशोदा नन्द श्री गोविन्द

अन्तरा- दीनानाथ दुख भंजन
पद नमामि मधुसूदन
वासुदेव वन माली
बृज पति यदु नन्द नन्दन

स्थाई-

प	मं	ग	ग	रे	ग	ध	प	ग	मं	ग	रे
पा	ऽ	र	ब्र	ऽ	ह्म	प	र	मे	ऽ	श्व	र
x		०		२		०		३		४	

ग	मं	प	-	ध	पमं	ग	मं	गरे	ग	रे	सा
पु	रु	षो	ऽ	त्त	मऽ	प	र	माऽ	नं	ऽ	द
x		०		२		०		३		४	

निं	-	ध	निं	सा	सा	सा	ग	रे	ग	-	ग
न	ऽ	न्द	न	न्द	न	आ	न	न्द	क	ऽ	न्द
x		०		२		०		३		४	

सां	निं	ध	निं	ध	प	प	-	मं	ग	रे	ग
य	शो	दा	न	ऽ	न्द	श्री	ऽ	गो	वि	ऽ	न्द
x		०		२		०		३		४	

अन्तरा-

ग	म॑	ध	सां	–	सां	सां	सां	सांनि	रें	सां	सां
दी	ना	ऽ	ना	ऽ	थ	दु	ख	भं ऽ	ऽ	ज	न
x		0		२		0		३		४	

नि	–	ध	नि	सां	सां	सां	रें	सां	नि	ध	प
प	ऽ	द	न	ऽ	मा	मि	म	ध्रु सू		द	न
x		0		२		0		३		४	

सां	गं	गं	मं	रें	सा	नि	सां	ध	–	प	–
वा	ऽ	सु	दे	ऽ	व	व	न	मा	ऽ	ली	ऽ
x		0		२		0		३		४	

ग	म॑	प	ध	नि	ध	प	–	म॑	म॑	रे	ग
बृ	ज	प	ति	य	दु	न	ऽ	न्द	न	न्द	न
x		0		२		0		३		४	

RAAG MARVA

thaat marva: sa re ga ma dha ni
swara: In this raag pa is not used, therefore this raag consists of only six
    swaras. Re is komal and ma is tivra.
jati: shadhav/shadhav   6/6
vadi swara: dha
samvadi swara: re
time of singing: evening
pakar: ni dha, ni re re ga ma dha dha ma ga, re re ni dha ˢ ni re sa
aroh: ni re ga ma dha ni sa
avaroh: sa ni dha ma ga re sa

alaap:

1. ni re ˢ ˢ ˢ sa ˢ ˢ ˢ ni dha ˢ ˢ ˢ ni re ˢ ˢ ˢ sa ˢ ˢ ˢ ni re ga re ˢ ˢ ˢ ni dha ˢ ˢ ˢ ni
re ˢ ˢ ˢ sa ˢ ˢ ˢ ˢ

2. ni dha ˢ ˢ ma dha ni re ˢ ˢ ˢ ga ˢ ˢ ˢ dha ni re ga re re sa ˢ ˢ ni re ga ma dha
ˢ ˢ ˢ ᵈʰᵃma ga ˢ re re sa ˢ ˢ ˢ

3. dha ni re re ga ma dha ˢ ˢ ˢ ˢ madhani dha ˢ ˢ ˢ ma dha ˢ ˢ ˢ maga re re ni
dha ˢ ˢ ˢ ni re sa ˢ ga ma dha ˢ ˢ ˢ ni ˢ ˢ ˢ re ni dha ˢ ˢ ma dha ˢ ˢ ˢ ma ga ˢ ˢ
dha ˢ ˢ ma ga re sa ˢ ˢ ˢ ˢ

4. ni re ga ma dha ˢ ˢ ˢ ˢ ma dha ni re ˢ ˢ ˢ sa ˢ ˢ ni dha ˢ ˢ ˢ ˢ ma dha ˢ ˢ ˢ ˢ
ma ga re re sa ˢ ˢ ˢ ˢ

5. ni re ni dha ˢ ˢ ˢ ma ga ˢ ˢ ma dha ni ˢ ˢ ni re ga ma dha ˢ ˢ ˢ ma dha ˢ ˢ ga
ma dha ni re ni dha ˢ ˢ ma dha ni re sa ˢ ˢ ˢ ˢ reresani dha ˢ ˢ ma dha ˢ ˢ ˢ
dha ma ga re re sa ˢ ˢ ˢ

RAAG MARVA (Ek Taal)

sthayi: Shyaama sundara madana mohana
Natavara giradhaaree
Rahata rahata karata raara
Mose banavaaree

antara: Meethee meethee baata karata
Kachhu kee para baanha dharata
Panaghata na jaane deta
Shira gagaree bhaaree

sthayi:

maˈdha –	maˈ	ga	re	ga	re	ga	maˈ	ga	maˈ	ga
shyaaꜱ ꜱ	ma	sun	da	ra	ma	da	na	mo	ha	na
x	0		2		0		3		4	

ni	reˑ	ni	dha	maˈ	ga	ni	dha	maˈ	ga	re	sa
na	ta	va	ra	gi	ra	dha ꜱ		ꜱ ꜱ		ree	ꜱ
x		0		2		0		3		4	

niˌ	niˌ	re	ga	maˈ	ga	dha	maˈ	dha	saˈ	–	saˈ
ra	ha	ta	ra	ha	ta	ka	ra	ta	raa	ꜱ	ra
x		0		2		0		3		4	

nireˑ	–	nidha	maˈga	dha	maˈ	ni	dha	maˈ	ga	re	sa
moꜱ	ꜱ	seꜱ	ꜱꜱ	ba	na	vaa	ꜱ	ꜱ	ꜱ	ree	ꜱ
x		0		2		0		3		4	

antara:

maॱ	–	ga	maॱ	dha	ma	saॱ	–	saॱ	saॱ	saॱ	saॱ
mee	ꜱ	thee	mee	ꜱ	thee	baa	ꜱ	na	ka	ra	ta
x		0		2		0		3		4	

ni	rė	garė	–	saॱ	saॱ	ni	saॱ	rė	ni	dha	dha
ka	chhu	keeꜱ	ꜱ	pa	ra	baan	ꜱ	ha	dha	ra	ta
x		0		2		0		3		4	

maॱ	ni	dha	maॱ	ga	–	re	–	ga	maॱ	–	ga
pa	na	gha	ta	na	ꜱ	jaa	ꜱ	ne	de	ꜱ	ta
x		0		2		0		3		4	

ni	re	ga	maॱ	dha	maॱ	ni	dha	maॱ	ga	re	sa
shi	ra	ga	ga	ree	ꜱ	bhaa	ꜱ	ꜱ	ꜱ	ree	ꜱ
x		0		2		0		3		4	

राग मारवा

थाठ मारवा- सा रे॒ ग म॑ ध नि

स्वर-इस राग में रिषभ कोमल तथा मध्यम तीव्र का प्रयोग होता है, बाकी के शुद्ध स्वरों का प्रयोग होता है। इस राग में पंचम स्वर वर्जित है।

जाति- षाढव/षाढव ६/६

वादी-धैवत

सम्वादी-रिषभ

गायन का समय-सायंकाल

पकड़-नि॒ ध, नि॒ रे॒ रे॒ ग म॑ ध ध म ग, रे॒ रे॒ नि॒ ध ऽ नि॒ रे॒ सा

आरोह-नि॒ रे॒ ग म॑ ध नि सां

अवरोह-सां नि ध म॑ ग रे॒ सा

आलाप-

१. नि॒ रे॒ ऽ ऽ ऽ सा ऽ ऽ ऽ नि॒ ध ऽ ऽ ऽ नि॒ रे॒ ऽ ऽ ऽ सा ऽ ऽ ऽ ऽ नि॒ रे॒ ग रे॒ ऽ ऽ ऽ नि॒ ध ऽ ऽ नि॒ रे॒ ऽ ऽ ऽ सा ऽ ऽ ऽ ऽ

२. नि॒ ध ऽ ऽ म॑ ध नि॒ रे॒ ऽ ऽ ऽ ग ऽ ऽ ऽ ध नि॒ रे॒ ग रे॒ रे॒ सा ऽ ऽ नि॒ रे॒ ग म॑ ध ऽ ऽ ऽ म॑ ग ऽ रे॒ रे॒ सा ऽ ऽ ऽ

३. ध नि॒ रे॒ रे॒ ग म॑ ध ऽ ऽ ऽ ऽ म॑ध नि ध ऽ ऽ ऽ म॑ ध ऽ ऽ ऽ ऽ म॑ग रे॒ रे॒ नि॒ ध ऽ ऽ ऽ नि॒ रे॒ सा ग म॑ ध ऽ ऽ ऽ नि॒ रें॒ नि॒ ध ऽ ऽ म॑ ध ऽ ऽ ऽ म॑ ग ऽ ध ध ऽ ऽ म॑ ग रे॒ सा ऽ ऽ ऽ

४. नि॒ रे॒ ग म॑ ध ध ऽ ऽ ऽ म॑ ध नि॒ रें॒ ऽ ऽ ऽ सां ऽ ऽ नि॒ ध ऽ ऽ ऽ ऽ म॑ ध ऽ ऽ ऽ ऽ म॑ ग रे॒ रे॒ सां ऽ ऽ ऽ

५. नि॒ रे॒ नि॒ ध ऽ ऽ ऽ म॑ग ऽ ऽ म॑ ध नि॒ ऽ ऽ नि॒ रे॒ ग म॑ ध ऽ ऽ ऽ म॑ ध ऽ ग म॑ ध नि रें॒ नि॒ ध ऽ ऽ म॑ ध नि रें॒ सां ऽ ऽ ऽ ऽ रें॒रें॒सांनि॒ ध ऽ ऽ म॑ ध ऽ ऽ ध म॑ ग रे॒ रे॒ सा ऽ ऽ ऽ

राग मारवा   (एक ताल)

स्थाई   श्याम सुन्दर मदन मोहन
          नटवर गिरधारी
          रहत रहत करत रार
          मोसे बनवारी

अन्तरा-   मीठी मीठी बात करत
          कछु की पर बाँह धरत
          पनघट न जाने देत
          शिर गगरी भारी

स्थाई-

अन्तरा-

	म॑	-	ग	म॑	ध	म॑	सां	-	सां	सां	सां	सां
	मी	ऽ	ठी	मी	ऽ	ठी	बा	ऽ	त	क	र	त
	x		०		२		०		३		४	

	नि	रें॒	गरें॑	-	सां	सां	नि	सां	रें॒	नि	ध	ध
	क	छु	कीऽ	ऽ	प	र	बाँ	ऽ	ह	ध	र	त
	x		०		२		०		३		४	

	म॑	नि	ध	म॑	ग	-	रे॒	-	ग	म॑	-	ग
	प	न	घ	ट	न	ऽ	जा	ऽ	ने	दे	ऽ	त
	x		०		२		०		३		४	

	नि॒	रे॒	ग	म॑	ध	म॑	नि	ध	म॑	ग	रे॒	सा
	शि	र	ग	ग	री	ऽ	भा	ऽ	ऽ	ऽ	री	ऽ
	x		०		२		०		३		४	

RAAG PURVI

thaat purvi: sa re ga ma pa dha ni

swara: In this raag both kinds of ma (shuddh and tivra) as well as komal re and dha are used.

jati: sampurn/sampurn   7/7

vadi swara: ga

samvadi swara: ni

time of singing: evening

pakar: dha pa ma ga ma ga re ma ga ᵐᵃ re sa

aroh: ni re ga ma pa dha ni sa

avaroh: sa ni dha pa ma pa, ga ma ga, re sa

alaap:

1. sa ꜱ ꜱ ꜱ ni re sa ꜱ ꜱ ꜱ ni re ga ma ga ꜱ ꜱ ꜱ re sa ꜱ ꜱ ꜱ ni re ga ma ꜱ ꜱ ꜱ pamagamaga ꜱ ꜱ ꜱ ma ga re sa

2. ni re ga ꜱ ꜱ ꜱ ma ga ꜱ ꜱ re sa ꜱ ꜱ ꜱ ni re ga ma pa ꜱ ꜱ ma pa ga ma ga ꜱ ꜱ ꜱ ni re ga ma pa ꜱ ꜱ ꜱ ma pa ga ma ga ꜱ ꜱ ma ga re sa ꜱ ꜱ ꜱ ꜱ

3. ni re ga ma pa ꜱ ꜱ ꜱ pamadhapa ꜱ ꜱ ꜱ ga ma ga ꜱ ꜱ ꜱ ꜱ ga ma dha pa ꜱ ꜱ ma dha ni ꜱ ꜱ dha pa ꜱ ꜱ ꜱ ga ma ga ꜱ ꜱ ꜱ ma ga ꜱ ꜱ re ꜱ sa ꜱ ꜱ ꜱ

4. ni re ga ma pa ꜱ ꜱ ma ga ꜱ ꜱ ma dha ni ꜱ ꜱ re ni dha ꜱ ꜱ pa ꜱ ꜱ ꜱ ga ma ga ꜱ ꜱ ꜱ ma ga re sa ꜱ ꜱ ni re ga ma ꜱ pa ꜱ ꜱ ma ga ma dha ni re sa ꜱ ꜱ ꜱ re ni dha ꜱ ꜱ pa ꜱ ꜱ ma pa ga ma ga ꜱ ꜱ ꜱ ꜱ re sa ꜱ ꜱ

5. ga ma dha pa ga ma ga ꜱ ꜱ ꜱ ꜱ ni re ga ma pa ma pa ma dha pa ꜱ ꜱ ma dha ni re sa ꜱ ꜱ ꜱ ni re ga ma re sa ni dha pa ꜱ ꜱ ꜱ dha ma pa ga ma ga ꜱ ꜱ ma ga re sa

RAAG PURVI   (Tri Taal)

sthayi: Aaye nahee giradhaaree
Baata takata moree akhiyaan haaree

antara: Deepa liye mandira aayee
Poojana archana le lo maaee
Haatha joda ye vinatee hamaaree
Bhejo more mohana muraaree

sthayi:

															ni
															aa
re	gama	pa	ma	dha	pa	-	-	pa	dha	ma	pama	ga	ma	ga,	ma
s	ye s	s	na	hee	s	s	s	gi	ra	dhaa	ss	ree	s	s,	baa
3				x				2				0			
ga	re	re	sa	re	re	sa	ni	re	gama	pa	ga	pama	gare	sa,	ni
s	ta	ta	ka	ta	mo	ree	a	khi	yaan s	s	haa	ss	ss	ree,	aa
3				x				2				0			

antara:

```
ma  ga   ma  dha | sa  sa  -   sa | ni   dha  nire  ni | dha  pa  -   -
dee ꜱ    pa  ꜱ   | li  ye  ꜱ   ma | ndi  ra   aaꜱ   ꜱ  | yee  ꜱ   ꜱ,  ꜱ
3                | x              | 2                  | 0


pa  dha  ma  pa | ma  dha  sa  sa | nire  ga  re  sa | re   ni  dha  pa
poo ꜱ    ja  na | ar  ꜱ    cha na | leꜱ   ꜱ   lo  ꜱ  | maa  ꜱ   ee   ꜱ
3               | x               | 2                | 0


ma  dha  sa  sa | -   sa  sa  sa | ni  re  ga   re | sa   ni  dha  pa
haa ꜱ    tha jo | ꜱ   da  ye  ꜱ  | vi  na  tee  ha | maa  ꜱ   ree  ꜱ
3               | x              | 2               | 0


dha  dha  pa  ma | pa  ga  ma  ga | re  ni  re   - | sa   -   -,   ni
bhe  ꜱ    jo  mo | re  mo  ꜱ   ha | na  mu  raa  ꜱ | ree  ꜱ   ꜱ,   aa
3                | x              | 2              | 0
```

राग पूर्वी

थाठ पूर्वी- सा रे॒ ग म॑ प ध॒ नि

स्वर-इस राग में मध्यम दोनों तथा रिषव और धैवत कोमल स्वर लगते हैं।

जाति-सम्पूर्ण/सम्पूर्ण   ७/७

वादी-गंधार

सम्वादी-निशाद

गायन समय- सायंकाल

पकड़-ध॒ प म॑ ग म ग रे॒ म ग म॑ग रे॒ सा

आरोह-नि॒ रे॒ ग म॑ प ध॒ नि सां

अवरोह-सां नि ध॒ प म॑ प, ग म ग, रे॒ सा

आलाप-

१. सा ऽ ऽ ऽ नि॒ रे॒ सा ऽ ऽ ऽ नि॒ रे॒ ग म ग ऽ ऽ ऽ रे॒ सा ऽ ऽ ऽ नि॒ रे॒ ग म॑ ऽ ऽ ऽ प॑मगमग ऽ ऽ ऽ म॑ ग रे॒ सा

२. नि॒ रे॒ ग ऽ ऽ ऽ म॑ ग ऽ ऽ रे॒ सा ऽ ऽ ऽ नि॒ रे॒ ग म॑ ऽ ऽ ऽ प ऽ ऽ ऽ म॑ प ग म ग ऽ ऽ ऽ नि॒ रे॒ ग म॑ प ऽ ऽ ऽ म॑ प ग म

   ग ऽ ऽ म॑ ग रे॒ सा ऽ ऽ ऽ ऽ

३. नि॒ रे॒ ग म॑ प ऽ ऽ ऽ प॑म॑ध॒प ऽ ऽ ऽ ग म ग ऽ ऽ ऽ ऽ ग म॑ ध॒ प ऽ ऽ म॑ ध॒ नि ऽ ऽ ध॒ प ऽ ऽ ऽ ग म ग ऽ ऽ ऽ म॑ ग

   रे॒ ऽ रे॒ सा ऽ ऽ ऽ

४. नि॒ रे॒ ग म॑ प ऽ ऽ म॑ ग ऽ ऽ म॑ ध॒ नि ऽ ऽ रें॒ नि ध॒ ऽ ऽ प ऽ ऽ ऽ ग म ग ऽ ऽ म॑ ग रे॒ सा ऽ नि॒ रे॒ ग म॑ प ऽ ऽ

   म॑ ग म॑ ध॒ नि रें॒ सां ऽ ऽ ऽ रें॒ नि ध॒ ऽ ऽ प ऽ ऽ म॑ प ग म ग ऽ ऽ ऽ रे॒ सा ऽ ऽ

५. ग म॑ ध॒ प ग म ग ऽ ऽ ऽ ऽ नि॒ रे॒ ग म॑ प म॑ प म॑ ध॒ प ऽ ऽ म॑ ध॒ नि रें॒ सां ऽ ऽ ऽ नि॒ रें॒ गं म॑ं रे॒ सा नि ध॒ प ऽ ऽ ऽ

   ध॒ म॑ प ग म ग ऽ ऽ म॑ ग रे॒ सा

91

राग पूर्वी   (त्रिताल)

स्थाई आये नहीं गिरधारी
   बाट तकत मोरी अखियाँ हारी

अन्तरा दीप लिए मन्दिर आई
   पूजन अर्चन ले लो माई
   हाथ जोड़ ये विनती हमारी
   भेजो मोरे मोहन मुरारी

स्थाई-

															नि॒
															आ

रे॒	गम॑	प	म॑	ध॒	प	-	-	प	ध॒	म॑	प॒म॑	ग	म	ग,	म॑
ऽ	येऽ	ऽ	न	हीं	ऽ	ऽ	ऽ	गि	र	धा	ऽऽ,	री	ऽ	ऽ,	बा
३				x				२			०				

ग	रे॒	रे॒	सा	रे॒	रे॒	सा	नि॒	रे॒	गम॑	प	ग	प॒म॑	गरे॒	सा,	नि
ऽ	ट	त	क	तं	मो	री	अ	खि	याँऽ	ऽ	हा	ऽऽ,	ऽऽ,	री,	आ
३				x				२				०				

अन्तरा-

म॑	ग	म॑	ध॒	सां	सां	-	सां	नि	ध॒	निरें	नि	ध॒	प	-,	-
दी	ऽ	प	ऽ	लि	ये	ऽ	म	न्दि	र	आऽ	ऽ	ई	ऽ	ऽ,	ऽ
३				x				२				०			

प	ध॒	म॑	प	म॑	ध॒	सां	सां	निरें	गं	रें	सां	रें	नि	ध॒	प
पू	ऽ	ज	न	अ	ऽ	र्च	न	लेऽ	लो	ऽ	ऽ	मा	ऽ	ई	ऽ
३				x				२				०			

म॑	ध॒	सां	सां	-	सां	सां	सां	नि	रें	गं	रें	सां	नि	ध॒	प
हा	ऽ	थ	जो	ऽ	ड़	ये	ऽ	वि	न	ती	ह	मा	ऽ	री	ऽ
३				x				२				०			

ध॒	ध॒	प	म॑	प	ग	म	ग	रें	निं	रें	-	सा	-	-,	निं
भे	ऽ	जो	मो	रे	मो	ऽ	ह	न	मु	रा	ऽ	री	ऽ	ऽ,	आ
३				x				२				०			

RAAG TODI

thaat todi: sa re̲ ga̲ má pa dha̲ ni

swara: This raag consists of all seven swaras. Re, ga, and dha are komal, and ma is tivra.

jati: shadhav/sampurn   6/7

vadi swara: dha̲

samvadi swara: ga̲

time of singing: second part of the day

pakar: ⁿⁱdha̲, ni re̲ ga̲, ᵐᵃ re̲ ga̲ re̲ sa

aroh: sa re̲ ga̲ má pa dha̲ ni sȧ

avaroh: sȧ ni dha̲ pa má dha̲ má re̲ ga̲ re̲ sa

alaap:

1. sa ꞩ ꞩ re̲ ꞩ ꞩ ꞩ re̲ ga̲ re̲ ꞩ ꞩ ꞩ sa ꞩ ꞩ ꞩ sa ni dha̲ ꞩ ꞩ ꞩ ni sȧ sa ꞩ ꞩ ꞩ re̲ ga̲ ꞩ re̲ ꞩ ꞩ
   sa ꞩ ꞩ sa re̲ ga̲ ꞩ ꞩ ꞩ ᵐᵃre̲ ga̲ ꞩ ꞩ re sa ꞩ ꞩ ꞩ ꞩ

2. dha̲ ni sa re̲ ga̲ ꞩ ꞩ ꞩ ꞩ ˢᵃre̲ ꞩ ꞩ ꞩ re̲ ga̲ re̲ ꞩ ꞩ ꞩ sa ꞩ ꞩ sa re̲ ꞩ ꞩ ꞩ ga̲ ꞩ ꞩ re̲ ga̲
   má ꞩ ꞩ ꞩ ꞩ ᵖᵃmá ꞩ ꞩ ꞩ ga̲ ꞩ ꞩ ꞩ re̲ ga̲ ꞩ ꞩ ꞩ re̲ ꞩ ꞩ ꞩ sa ꞩ ꞩ ꞩ ꞩ ꞩ ˢᵃdha̲ ꞩ ꞩ ꞩ ni ꞩ ꞩ
   sa ꞩ ꞩ ꞩ re̲ ga̲ ꞩ ꞩ ꞩ ᵐᵃre̲ ꞩ ꞩ ꞩ ga̲ re̲ sa ꞩ ꞩ ꞩ ꞩ

3. sa re̲ ga̲ ꞩ ꞩ ꞩ ꞩ ꞩ má dha̲ ꞩ ꞩ ꞩ má ga̲ ꞩ ꞩ ꞩ re̲ ꞩ ꞩ ꞩ ga̲ má ꞩ ꞩ dha̲ ꞩ ꞩ ꞩ pa ꞩ
   ꞩ ꞩ má ga̲ re̲ ꞩ ꞩ ꞩ ga̲ ꞩ ꞩ re̲ sa ꞩ ꞩ ꞩ sa re̲ ga̲ ꞩ ꞩ ꞩ má dha̲ ni ꞩ ꞩ dha̲ ꞩ ꞩ ꞩ

   pa ꞩ ꞩ ꞩ ga̲ ꞩ ꞩ má dha̲ ꞩ ꞩ ꞩ ni sȧ ꞩ ꞩ ꞩ ꞩ re̲ ga̲ re̲ ꞩ ꞩ sa ꞩ ꞩ ꞩ ni dha̲ pa ꞩ ꞩ ꞩ
   dha̲ má ga̲ ꞩ ꞩ ꞩ re̲ ga̲ re̲ ꞩ ꞩ sa ꞩ

RAAG TODI (Dhruvapada) (Char Taal)

sthayi: Veda ratat brahma ratat
                Shesha ratat shambhu ratat
                Naarada muni vyaasa ratat
                Paavat nahi paara jako

antara: Gangaa gana gesh ratat
                Dhruva jana prahlaada ratat
                Gautam kee naara ratat
                Kaartik kumaar ratat

sthayi:

dha	pa	ma	ga	ga	ga	re	ga	re	sa	sa	sa
ve	S	da	ra	ta	ta	bra	S	hma	ra	ta	t
x		0		2		0		3		4	

sa	ni	dha	ni	sa	sa	re	ga	ga	sa	sa	sa
sha	S	sha	ra	ta	t	sha	S	mbhu	ra	ta	t
x		0		2		0		3		4	

re	dha	pa	pa	ma	dha	dha	ni	dha	dha	dha	pa
naa	S	ra	da	mu	ni	vyaa	S	sa	ra	ta	t
x		0		2		0		3		4	

dhani	sa	ni	dha	pa	ma	re	ga	re	re	sa	sa
paS	S	va	ta	na	hi	paa	S	ra	ja	S	ko
x		0		2		0		3		4	

95

antara:

re	dha	ni	sa	sa	sa	re	ga	ga	re	sa	sa
gan	ꜱ	gaa	ꜱ	ga	na	ge	sh	ꜱ	ra	ta	t
x		0		2		0		3		4	

re	ga	ga	ga	re	ga	re	ga	ma	re	ga	sa
dhu	va	ja	na	pra	ha	laa	ꜱ	da	ra	ta	t
x		0		2		0		3		4	

ni	ni	dha	dha	pa	pa	ma	dha	ni	ni	dha	dha
gau	ꜱ	ta	m	kee	ꜱ	naa	ꜱ	ra	ra	ta	t
x		0		2		0		3		4	

dhani	sa	ni	dha	pa	ma	re	ga	re	re	sa	sa
kaaꜱ	ꜱ	tir	ke	ꜱ	ku	maa	ꜱ	ra	ra	ta	t
x		0		2		0		3		4	

राग तोड़ी

थाठ-तोड़ी-सा <u>रे</u> <u>ग</u> ⁺म प <u>ध</u> नि

स्वर-इस राग में रिषभ, गंधार, धैवत कोमल तथा मध्यम तीव्र लगता है। बाकी के शुद्ध स्वरों का प्रयोग होता है।

जाति-षाडव/सम्पूर्ण   ६/७

वादी-धैवत

सम्वादी-गंधार

गाने का समय-दिन का दूसरा प्रहर

पकड़-^{नि}<u>ध</u>, नि <u>रे</u> <u>ग</u>, ⁺<u>रे</u> <u>ग</u> <u>रे</u> सा

आरोह-सा <u>रे</u> <u>ग</u> ⁺म <u>ध</u> नि सां

अवरोह-सां नि <u>ध</u> प ⁺म <u>ध</u> ⁺म <u>रे</u> <u>ग</u> <u>रे</u> सा

आलाप-

१. सा ऽ ऽ <u>रे</u> ऽ ऽ ऽ <u>रे</u> <u>ग</u> <u>रे</u> ऽ ऽ ऽ सा ऽ ऽ ऽ सा नि <u>ध</u> ऽ ऽ ऽ नि ऽ सा ऽ ऽ ऽ <u>रे</u> <u>ग</u> <u>रे</u> <u>रे</u> ऽ सा ऽ ऽ सा ऽ <u>रे</u> <u>ग</u> ऽ ऽ ऽ ⁺<u>रे</u> <u>ग</u> ऽ ऽ <u>रे</u> सा ऽ ऽ ऽ ऽ

२. <u>ध</u> नि सा <u>रे</u> <u>ग</u> ऽ ऽ ऽ ऽ ^{सां}<u>रे</u> ऽ ऽ ऽ <u>रे</u> <u>ग</u> <u>रे</u> ऽ ऽ ऽ सा ऽ ऽ सा <u>रे</u> ऽ ऽ ऽ <u>ग</u> ऽ ऽ <u>रे</u> <u>ग</u> ⁺म ऽ ऽ ऽ ऽ ⁺म ऽ ऽ ऽ <u>ग</u> ऽ ऽ ऽ <u>रे</u> <u>ग</u> ऽ ऽ ऽ <u>रे</u> ऽ ऽ सा ऽ ऽ ऽ ऽ ऽ ^{सां}<u>ध</u> ऽ ऽ ऽ नि ऽ ऽ सा ऽ ऽ ऽ <u>रे</u> <u>ग</u> ऽ ऽ ऽ ⁺<u>रे</u> ऽ ऽ ऽ <u>ग</u> <u>रे</u> सां ऽ ऽ ऽ ऽ

३. सा <u>रे</u> <u>ग</u> ऽ ऽ ऽ ऽ ऽ ⁺म <u>ध</u> ऽ ऽ ऽ ⁺म <u>ग</u> ऽ ऽ ऽ <u>रे</u> ऽ ऽ ऽ <u>ग</u> ⁺म ऽ ऽ <u>ध</u> ऽ ऽ ऽ प ऽ ऽ ऽ ⁺म <u>ग</u> <u>रे</u> ऽ ऽ ऽ <u>ग</u> ऽ ऽ <u>रे</u> सा ऽ ऽ ऽ सा <u>रे</u> <u>ग</u> ऽ ऽ ऽ ⁺म <u>ध</u> नि ऽ ऽ <u>ध</u> ऽ ऽ ऽ प ऽ ऽ ऽ <u>ग</u> ऽ ऽ ⁺म <u>ध</u> ऽ ऽ ऽ नि सां ऽ ऽ ऽ <u>रें</u> <u>गं</u> <u>रे</u> ऽ ऽ सां ऽ ऽ ऽ नि <u>ध</u> प ऽ ऽ ऽ <u>ध</u> ⁺म <u>ग</u> ऽ ऽ ऽ <u>रे</u> <u>ग</u> <u>रे</u> ऽ ऽ सा ऽ

राग तोड़ी (ध्रुवपद) (चार ताल)

स्थाई वेद रटत ब्रह्म रटत

शेष रटत शम्भु रटत

नारद मुनि व्यास रटत

पावत नहि पार जाको

अन्तरा गंगा गन गेश रटत

ध्रुब जन प्रह्लाद रटत

गौतम की नार रटत

कार्तिक कुमार रटत

स्थाई-

ध	प	मं	ग	ग	ग	रे	ग	रे	सा	सा	सा
वे	ऽ	द	र	ट	त	ब्र	ऽ	ह्म	र	ट	त
x		०		२		०		३		४	

सा	नि	ध	नि	सा	सा	रे	ग	ग	सा	सा	सा
शे	ऽ	ष	र	ट	त	श	ऽ	म्भु	र	ट	त
x		०		२		०		३		४	

रे	ध	प	प	मं	ध	ध	नि	ध	ध	ध	प
ना	ऽ	र	द	मु	नि	व्या	ऽ	स	र	ट	त
x		०		२		०		३		४	

धनि	सां	नि	ध	प	मं	रे	ग	रे	रे	सा	सा
पाऽ	ऽ	व	त	न	हि	पा	ऽ	र	जा	ऽ	को
x		०		२		०		३		४	

अन्तरा-

रे	ध	नि	सां	सां	सां	रें	गं	गं	रें	सां	सां
गं	ऽ	गा	ऽ	ग	न	गे	श	ऽ	र	ट	त
x		०		२		०		३		४	

रें	गं	गं	गं	रें	गं	रें	गं	में	रें	गं	सां
धू	व	ज	न	प्र	ह	ला	ऽ	द	र	ट	त
x		०		२		०		३		४	

नि	नि	ध	ध	प	प	में	ध	नि	नि	ध	ध
गौ	ऽ	त	म	की	ऽ	ना	ऽ	र	र	ट	त
x		०		२		०		३		४	

धनि	सां	नि	ध	प	में	रे	ग	रे	रे	सा	सा
काऽ	ऽ	र्ति	क	ऽ	कु	मा	ऽ	र	र	ट	त
x		०		२		०		३		४	

99

CHAPTER FIVE

TWELVE CLASSICAL TAALS (RHYTHMS)

As we indicated earlier, the organization of the rhythmic element in Indian music is called taal. There are many distinct taals (or rhythmic patterns) and they are frequently very complex. The rhythm element of Indian music is difficult to learn from books alone, and here especially, study with a skilled music teacher is advised. To make sense of the following diagrams, the student will need to have studied the terms and definitions in the previous chapters carefully.

The main taals used will be given in this chapter. The following diagrams illustrate the main taals, showing the matras, sam, talis, and khalis, and the *bols* that correspond to each matra (the mnemonic names of the beats derived from playing the tabla). The diagrams also show the division of the taal into vibhags.

These rhythms or beats are counted in a particular fashion. In practice, sam and the talis each receive a clap of the right hand into the upturned left hand. On the khali matras, the right hand is turned up and an empty beat indicated in the air just to the right of the left hand.

In Indian music, it is the instrument called the *tabla* that is the most important element in helping to maintain the rhythm of a piece. Study of the tabla is very complex and subtle, and can really only be done under the guidance of an expert teacher. Some basic knowledge of the rhythmic element, however, is essential to all students of music.

Dadra Taal (6 matras or beats)

1	2	3	4	5	6
धा	धी	ना	धा	ती	ना
dha	dhi	na	dha	ti	na ·
x			0		

Rupak Taal (7 matras)

1	2	3	4	5	6	7
ती	ती	ना	धी	ना	धी	ना
ti	ti	na	dhi	na	dhi	na
0			2		3	
x						

Tivra Taal (7 matras)

1	2	3	4	5	6	7
धा	दिं	ता	तिट	कत	गदि	गिन
dha	din	ta	tita	kata	gadi	gina
x			2		3	

Teen Taal (16 matras)

1	2	3	4	5	6	7	8	9	10	11	12	13	14	15	16
धा	धिं	धिं	धा	धा	धिं	धिं	धा	धा	तिं	तिं	ता	ता	धिं	धिं	धा
dha	dhin	dhin	dha	dha	dhin	dhin	dha	dha	tin	tin	ta	ta	dhin	dhin	dha
x				2				0				3			

Jhap Taal (10 matras)

1	2	3	4	5	6	7	8	9	10
धी	ना	धी	धी	ना	ती	ना	धी	धी	ना
dhi	na	dhi	dhi	na	ti	na	dhi	dhi	na
x		2			0		3		

Ek Taal (12 matras)

1	2	3	4	5	6	7	8	9	10	11	12
धिं	धिं	धागे	तिरकित	तू	ना	क	त्ता	धागे	तिरकित	धी	ना
dhin	dhin	dhage	tirkit	tu	na	kat	ta	dhage	tirkit	dhi	na
x		0		2		0		3		4	

Char Taal (12 matras)

1	2	3	4	5	6	7	8	9	10	11	12
धा	धा	दिं	ता	किट	धा	धिं	ता	तिट	कति	गदि	गिन
dha	dha	din	ta	kita	dha	dhin	ta	tita	kati	gadi	gina
x		0		2		0		3		4	

Deep Chandi Taal (14 matras)

1	2	3	4	5	6	7	8	9	10	11	12	13	14
धा	धिं	-	धा	गे	ति	-	ता	तीं	-	धा	गे	धिं	-
dha	dhin	-	dha	ge	ti	-	ta	tin	-	dha	ge	dhin	-
x			2				0			3			

Kaharwa Taal (8 matras)

1	2	3	4	5	6	7	8
धा	गे	ना	ति	ना	क	धि	ना
dha	ge	na	ti	na	ka	dhi	na
x				0			

Tilvada Taal (16 matras)

1	2	3	4	5	6	7	8	9	10	11	12	13	14	15	16
धा	तिरकिट	धिं	धिं	धा	धा	धिं	धिं	ता	तिरकिट	धिं	धिं	धा	धा	धिं	धिं
dha	tirkit	dhin	dhin	dha	dha	dhin	dhin	ta	tirkit	dhin	dhin	dha	dha	dhin	dhin
x				2				0				3			

Ada Char Taal (14 matras)

1	2	3	4	5	6	7	8	9	10	11	12	13	14
धिं	तिरकिट	धी	ना	तू	ना	कत	ता	तिरकिट	धी	ना	धी	धी	ना
dhin	tirkit	dhi	na	tu	na	kat	ta	tirkit	dhi	na	dhi	dhi	na
x		2		0		3		0		4		0	

Sul Taal (10 matras)

1	2	3	4	5	6	7	8	9	10
धा	धा	दिं	ता	किट	धा	तिट	कत	गदि	गिन
dha	dha	din	ta	kita	dha	tita	kata	gadi	gina
x		0		2		3		0	

GLOSSARY

Abhinava Raga Manjari: A text on music.

Abhoga: In the ancient system of singing, there used to be four parts: sthayi, antara, sanchari, and abhoga. Dhrupad singing, today, still retains abhoga.

Achala: Unchanging; the two swaras, *sa* (1) and *pa* (5), are never raised or lowered, so they are never sharp or flat, but always shuddh or pure. Thus, they are unchanging and steady and are called achala.

Ahata nada: When the equilibrium of an object is disturbed (for example, by striking it, hitting it, shaking it, or rubbing it against another object), then sound is produced. Such sound, heard sound, is called ahata nada.

Alaap: When the swaras of the raag are presented in a slow tempo, and contemplative mood, it is called the alaap.

Alankar: A systematic arrangement of varnas that help a student to develop technical ability is called an alankar.

Anahata nada: In deep meditation, the yogi hears another type of nada. There is no sound in the external world that corresponds to this internal one. This eternal inner sound vibrates in space (akash) without apparent cause. It is called anahata nada.

Antara: In the ancient system of singing, there used to be four parts: sthayi, antara, sanchari, and abhoga. Antara is the verse of the song.

Anuvadi: The remaining less important swaras in a raag, aside from the vadi and samvadi swaras, are called anuvadi.

Aroh: Two or more swaras placed in ascending order.

Asavari: The name of both a thaat and a raag having no sharps and three flats, *ga, dha,* and *ni.*

Audav: An ascending or descending scale using only five of the seven possible notes in a raag.

Avaroh: Two or more swaras placed in descending order.

Avayava: Avayava literally means limb or part, which here refers to the parts of a song. In the ancient system of singing, there used to be four parts: sthayi, antara, sanchari, and abhoga.

Bhairav: The name of both a thaat and a raag having two flat notes, *re* and *dha* and no sharps; it uses all the notes of the scale both in ascent and descent. Its vadi swara is *dha* flat; its samvadi swara is *re* flat. It is usually played in the early morning.

Bhairavi: The name of both a thaat and a raag having four flats: komal *re, ga, dha* and *ni.*

Bhastrika: A breathing technique or pranayama to be used once diaphragmatic breathing is a natural and unconscious function. In bhastrika, attention is paid to the use of the diaphragm and abdominal muscles. The chest, shoulders, and facial muscles should remain relaxed. Bhastrika means "bellows." In this exercise the abdominal muscles move forcefully in and out like a blacksmith's bellows. In bhastrika both exhalation and inhalation are vigorous and forceful.

Bilawal: The name of both a thaat and a raag having no sharp or flat notes; all seven notes are used both in ascent and descent. Its vadi swara is *dha;* its samvadi swara is *ga.* It is sung in the morning.

GLOSSARY

Brahmari: A breathing technique or pranayama done by exhaling with a partially closed glottis so that the air is felt on the roof of the palate, reproducing the humming sound of a bee. Brahmari soothes the nerves and calms the mind.

Chala: The "changeable" swaras of the saptak which can be komal (flat) or tivra (sharp)—*re, ga, ma, dha,* and *ni.* These are "unsteady."

Chromatic scale: A scale including all of the twelve notes in an octave. On a piano, it is all of the black and white keys.

Crocodile pose: A relaxation posture in which one lies on the stomach, placing the legs a comfortable distance apart and pointing the toes outward. The arms are folded in front of the body, resting the hands on the upper arms and the forehead on the forearms. The elbows and lower arms are positioned so that the chest does not touch the floor. In this position, concentration is on the breath and the effect of diaphragmatic breathing.

Dadra: The taal which has six beats.

Dhrupad: An ancient singing style.

Diaphragmatic breathing: In this breathing technique, concentrate on the movement of the diaphragm. During inhalation the diaphragm contracts and flattens; it pushes downward, causing the upper abdominal muscles to relax and extend slightly and the lower "floating" ribs to flare slightly outward. In this position the lungs expand, creating a partial vacuum, which draws air into the chest cavity. During exhalation the diaphragm relaxes and returns to its dome-shaped position. During this upward movement, the upper abdominal muscles contract, and carbon dioxide is forced from the lungs.

Drut: In reference to rhythm, drut is fast.

Duration: Duration refers to the fact that sounds occur in time—they are either long or short.

Flats: Some swaras are komal (soft, or flat). That is, the pure swara has been changed by being lowered in pitch. This can be done with the swaras *re, ga, dha,* and *ni* only.

Hindustani music: The music of northern India, that is most widely known as "Indian" music around the world.

Jati: The classification of a raag based on the number of notes used in its ascending and descending scales. The classifications are: sampurn (pure, or using all seven notes), shadhav (using six of the seven notes), and audav (using five of the seven notes).

Kafi: The name of both a thaat and a raag having no sharps and two flats, *ga* and *ni;* all seven notes are used both in ascent and descent. Its vadi swara is *pa.* It is sung at about midnight.

Kalyan: The name of both a thaat and a raag. The thaat has one sharp (*ma*) and no flats. The raag is based on kalyan thaat, and uses all the notes in the descent, but starts on mandra *ni* and skips madhya *sa* on the ascent. Its vadi swara is *ga.* It is sung in the first part of the night, from about six to nine.

Kana swara: Grace note: the act of lightly touching upon a preceding or following swara in the act of playing or singing the main one.

Karnatic music: The music of southern India.

Khali: A taal consists of four main components: vibhag, tali, khali, and sam. The weakest matra in the taal is called khali, and is indicated in the notation with a '0.'

Khamaj: The name of both a thaat and a raag. The thaat has no sharps and one flat (*ni*). The raag uses *ni* flat only in the descent. It uses six notes in ascent (omitting *re*) and all seven notes in the descent. Its vadi swara is *ga.* It is sung in the second part of the night, from about nine to midnight.

Khanda Gayaki: A particular technique of applying swaras systematically.

GLOSSARY

Khataka: When three swaras are sung together in a rapid, circular motion it is called a khataka.

Komal: Some swaras are komal (soft, or flat). That is, the pure swara has been changed by being lowered in pitch. This can be done with the swaras *re, ga, dha,* and *ni.*

Lay: The tempo is the speed at which the taal is played and is called the lay. There are three main lays: vilambit, madhya, and drut.

Marva: The name of both a thaat and a raag having one sharp (*ma*) and one flat (*re*).

Madhya: In reference to rhythm, madhya is medium.

Madhya Saptak: The middle range: the swaras produced from this saptak resonate in the throat region. The sound of this range is neither too high nor too low.

Magnitude: The magnitude (or loudness) of a sound is the degree to which it can be heard at longer or shorter distances.

Major scale: When all seven swaras of a scale are natural or pure (or shuddh) they form a major scale.

Mandra Saptak: Lower range: the tones of this saptak are low and deep. Swaras produced from this saptak resonate in the heart region.

Matra: The Sanskrit word matra is related to the English word "meter." In music, both words are used in reference to the time element, the rhythm. A matra is the smallest unit of the measurement of time—a micro-moment, so to speak, a beat.

Meend: When a musician gracefully and tastefully slides through all the swaras of an interval (for example, from *sa* to *pa*) in an uninterrupted flow, that is called meend.

Mela: A progression using the various raised or lowered swaras of the saptak is called a thaat or mela.

Murki: When four or five swaras are sung together in a rapid, circular motion it is called a murki.

Nada: The word nada means "sound," that which is heard by the human ear. There are two types of nada; those that are pleasing to the ear or musical, and those that are dissonant and non-musical. Nada is sound produced through the regular and constant vibration of some object in space.

Nadi shodhanam: A breathing technique to purify the nadis, the subtle energy channels. It balances the flow of breath in the nostrils and the flow of energy in the nadis.

Octave: The common spatial arrangement of sound is the octave. An octave spans an interval of eight notes. This interval is created when the frequency of vibration of the highest note of the octave is exactly twice that of the lowest note.

Pakar: The most succinct arrangement of the swaras and the minimum number of swaras that must be sung to identify the raag is called the pakar.

Pitch: Pitch describes whether a sound is high or low.

Purvi: A thaat having one sharp (*ma*) and two flats (*re* and *dha*).

Purva raag (purvanga): A raag that has its vadi swara in the lower tetrachord is called a purva raag. The lower tetrachord is: *sa, re, ga, ma.*

Raag samaya: There is always an appropriate time to sing or play a particular raag, a time when the psychological effect of music on the mind will be most effective.

Raag: A melodic composition. It is composed within set rules and expresses a particular emotion.

GLOSSARY

Sam: A taal consists of four main components: vibhag, tali, khali, and sam. Generally, the first matra of the taal, which is usually the strongest matra rhythmically, is called sam. The sam is indicated on the diagram by an 'x.'

Sama Veda: An early scripture devoted to music.

Samchari varna: Combinations of the first three varnas, stationary, ascending, and descending, are called samchari.

Sampurn: An ascending or descending scale using all of the seven possible notes in a raag.

Samvadi: The second most frequently used swara in a particular raag is known as the samvadi swara.

Sanchari: One of the four parts of a piece according to the ancient system of singing.

Sangita Darpana: A text on music.

Sangita Ratnagar: A scripture devoted to Indian music, written by Sarangadev.

Saptak: The seven principle tones of a scale are called the saptak.

Scale: Within the octave are the seven notes (or twelve half-steps) of the scale—notes that are essentially shared by Indian and Western music. The theoretical ways of understanding and organizing the tones of the scale differ between East and West, however.

Shadaj: The lowest note of the three main octaves used by vocalists. It is the mother of all swaras.

Shadhav: An ascending or descending scale using only six of the seven possible notes in a raag.

Sharps: A swara can also be raised in pitch from its pure tone. Such a swara is tivra, or sharp. This can be done with the swara *ma*.

Shrutis: Microtones used in Indian music. They are divisions of the tones between the standard notes of the Western scale. There are twenty-two shrutis in an octave, in addition to the standard seven notes. It is the finest level of sound distinguishable by the meditative ear.

Shuddh swaras: When a swara is natural or pure it is termed shuddh.

Solfagio: The Western system of naming notes is called solfagio: do, re, mi, fa, sol, la, ti, (do).

Vikrit: When a shuddh note has been raised or lowered, sharped or flatted, it is then called vikrit.

Sthayi: In the ancient system of singing, the sthayi is the chorus.

Swara: A swara is a musical tone or note. When either a vocalist or instrumentalist produces a sound, it is a swara. Swaras are the audible tones of music.

Taal: The pattern of matras or beats which forms what in Western music is actually the meter, is called the taal in Indian music. There are many taals, and each taal is named.

Tali: While counting or singing, a clap of the hands on the strong matra of sam and/or the first matra of subsequent vibhags (except for the khali vibhag) is called tali.

Taan: Singing clusters of swaras in a raag in a fast tempo is called taan. Through taan, the musician expands the raag.

Taar Saptak: Taar Saptak (high range): the swaras of this saptak are high in pitch. They resonate in the region of the head.

Tanpura: A musical instrument with four or five strings, tuned to the pitch of the singer, and used both to provide a background drone and to help in keeping time.

GLOSSARY

Teentaal: The taal which has sixteen beats is called teentaal.

Tetrachords: The saptak or scale can be divided into two parts. These two parts are what are called in the West, the "tetrachords."

Thaat: A progression using the various raised or lowered swaras of the saptak is called a thaat or mela.

Theka: When this entire structure of the taal is organized for performance, it is technically called the theka.

Timbre: The quality of sound that distinguishes one person's voice from another's, or one instrument from another, even when singing or playing at the same pitch or loudness is called "timbre." It is the distinctive tone of that voice or instrument.

Tivra: A swara can also be raised in pitch from its pure tone. Such a swara is tivra, or sharp. This can be done with the swara *ma*.

Todi: The name of both a raag and a thaat having one sharp (*ma*) and three flats, *re, ga,* and *dha*.

Ujjayi: A breathing technique or pranayama, that is done by partially closing the glottis so that both the incoming and outgoing air is felt on the roof of the palate, making a soft continuous, sobbing sound with the breath. Ujjayi clears the nasal passages, soothes the nerves, and calms the mind.

Uttara raag (uttranga): A raag that has its vadi swara in the upper tetrachord is called an uttara raag. The upper tetrachord is: *pa, dha, ni, sa*.

Vadi: The particular swara that is most frequently used in a raag is called the vadi swara.

Varjita: A swara which cannot be used in a raag at any cost is called varjita swara.

Varna: Varna is the possible direction a melody can take in being composed of swaras that are higher, lower or the same as the previous swara. The movement of the singer's voice from one swara to another is what will eventually produce a melody.

Vibhag: Each section of a taal is called vibhag. The vertical lines demarcate the sections.

Vilambit: In reference to rhythm, vilambit is slow.

Vivadi: Swaras that cannot generally be used in a particular raag because they are dissonant or rather offensive to the ear are termed vivadi.

PRONUNCIATION GUIDE

Sanskrit or Hindi vowels are generally the same pure vowel sounds found in Italian, Spanish, or French. The consonants are generally pronounced as in English.

a   *fa*ther
ai   *ai*sle
au   s*au*erkr*au*t
b   *b*ut
bh   a*bh*or
ch   *ch*ur*ch*
chh chur*chh*ill
d   *d*ough (slightly toward the *th* sound of *th*ough)
dh   a*dh*ere (slightly toward the *theh* sound of brea*the h*ear)
e   pr*e*y
g   *g*o
gh   do*gh*ouse
h   *h*ot
i   pol*i*ce
j   *j*ump
jh   lod*ge h*ouse
k   *k*id
kh   wor*kh*orse
l   *l*ug
m   *m*ud

n	si*ng*
n	*n*o
p	*p*ub
ph	u*ph*ill
r	*r*un
sh	*sh*awl (pronounced with a slight whistle; German *sp*rechen)
s	*s*un
t	*t*omato
th	*Th*ailand
u	p*u*sh
v	*v*odka (midway between *w* and *v*)
y	*y*es

Vowels. Every vowel is either long or short. The dipthongs *e, ai, o,* and *au* are always long. The long form of a vowel is pronounced twice as long as the short form.

Consonants. Sanskrit or Hindi has many aspirated consonants, that is, consonants pronounced with a slight *h* sound: *bh, chh, dh, gh, jh, kh, ph, th.* These aspirated consonants should be pronounced distinctly.

Accentuation. There is no strong accentuation of syllables. The general rule is to stress the next-to-last syllable of a word, if that is long. A syllable is long if (*a*) it has a long vowel or (*b*) its vowel is followed by more than one consonant. If the next-to-last syllable of a word is short, then the syllable before that receives the stress.

APPENDIX B

SWARA LIPI (NOTATIONS)

The following are the standard notations as established by Pandit Vishnu Narayana Bhatkande.

1) Madhya saptak: There is no special sign to indicate medium scale. Example: sa re ga ma pa dha ni

2) Mandra saptka: Each octave below the medium range is indicated by a dot underneath the swara. Example: ṇi ḍha ṗa ṃa g̣a ṛe ṣa

3) Taar saptak: Each octave above the medium range is indicated by a dot above the swara. Example: ṡa ṙe ġa ṁa ṗa ḋha ṅi ṡa

4) Komal swara (flat note) is indicated by a line underneath the swara. Example: re ga dha ni

5) Tivra swara (sharp note) is indicated by a vertical line above the swara ma. Example: ma

6) Kana swara (grace note) is indicated by a small swara written above the main swara. Example: sa^re ^ga ma

7) Meend swara (bridge) is indicated by a slur or curve above the two swaras. Example: sa pa

8) Murki swara is indicated by parenthesis: (pa)

9) Lenghtening the duration of the note is indicated by a dash after the swara. Example: sa - - -

10) Lengthening the syllable of the word is indicated by S after the syllable. Example: shya S S S

11) Two or more swaras in one matra are indicated by a curve underneath the swaras. Example: dhapa maga

12) Sam is indicated by an "x" underneath the first matra.

13) Khali is indicated by a "0" underneath the matra.

ABOUT THE AUTHOR

Yogi, scientist, philosopher, humanitarian, and mystic poet, Swami Rama is the founder and spiritual head of the Himalayan International Institute of Yoga Science and Philosophy, with its headquarters in Honesdale, Pennsylvania, and therapy and educational centers throughout the world. He was born in a Himalayan valley of Uttar Pradesh, India, in 1925 and was initiated and anointed in early childhood by a great sage of the Himalayas. He studied with many adepts, and then traveled to Tibet to study with his grandmaster. From 1949 to 1952 he held the prestige and dignity of Shankaracharya (spiritual leader) in Karvirpitham in the South of India. He then returned to the Himalayas to intensify his meditative practices in the cave monasteries and to establish an ashram in Rishikesh.

Later he continued his investigation of Western psychology and philosophy at several European universities, and he taught in Japan before coming to the United States in 1969. The following year he served as a consultant to the Voluntary Controls Project of the Research Department of the Menninger Foundation. There he demonstrated, under laboratory conditions, precise control over his autonomic nervous system and brain. The findings of that research increased the scientific community's understanding of the human ability to control autonomic functioning and to attain previously unrecognized levels of consciousness.

Shortly thereafter, Swami Rama founded the Himalayan Institute as a means to synthesize the ancient teachings of the East with the modern approaches of the West. He has played a major role in bringing the insights of yoga psychology and philosophy to the attention of the physicians and psychologists of the West. He continues to teach students around the world while intensifying his writing and meditative practices. He is the author of many books and currently spends most of his time in the mountains of Northern India and in Pennsylvania, U.S.A.

The main building of the national headquarters, Honesdale, Pa.

The Himalayan Institute

Since its establishment in 1971, the Himalayan Institute has been dedicated to helping individuals develop themselves physically, mentally, and spiritually, as well as contributing to the transformation of society. All the Institute programs—educational, therapeutic, research—emphasize holistic health, yoga, and meditation as tools to help achieve those goals. Institute programs combine the best of ancient wisdom and modern science, of Eastern teachings and Western technologies. We invite you to join with us in this ongoing process of personal growth and development.

Our beautiful national headquarters, on a wooded 400-acre campus in the Pocono Mountains of northeastern Pennsylvania, provides a peaceful, healthy setting for our seminars, classes, and training programs in the principles and practices of holistic living. Students from around the world have joined us here to attend programs in such diverse areas as biofeedback and stress reduction, hatha yoga, meditation, diet and nutrition, philosophy and metaphysics, and practical psychology for better living. We see the realization of our human potentials as a lifelong quest, leading to increased health, creativity, happiness, awareness, and improving the quality of life.

The Institute is a nonprofit organization. Your membership in the Institute helps to support its programs. Please call or write for information on becoming a member.

Institute Programs, Services, and Facilities

All Institute programs share an emphasis on conscious, holistic living and personal self-development. You may enjoy any of a number of diverse programs, including:

• Special weekend or extended seminars to teach skills and techniques for increasing your ability to be healthy and enjoy life
  • Holistic health services
  • Professional training for health professionals
  • Meditation retreats and advanced meditation instruction
  • Cooking and nutritional training
  • Hatha yoga and exercise workshops
  • Residential programs for self-development

The Himalayan Institute Charitable Hospital

A major aspect of the Institute's work around the world is its support of the construction and management of a modern, comprehensive hospital and holistic health facility in the mountain area of Dehra Dun, India. Outpatient facilities are already providing medical care to those in need, and mobile units have been equipped to visit outlying villages. Construction work on the main hospital building is progressing as scheduled.

We welcome financial support to help with the construction and the provision of services. We also welcome donations of medical supplies, equipment, or professional expertise. If you would like further information on the Hospital, please contact us.

Himalayan Institute Publications

Art of Joyful Living	Swami Rama
Book of Wisdom (Ishopanishad)	Swami Rama
A Call to Humanity	Swami Rama
Celestial Song/Gobind Geet	Swami Rama
Choosing a Path	Swami Rama
The Cosmic Drama: Bichitra Natak	Swami Rama
Enlightenment Without God	Swami Rama
Exercise Without Movement	Swami Rama
Freedom from the Bondage of Karma	Swami Rama
Indian Music, Volume I	Swami Rama
Inspired Thoughts of Swami Rama	Swami Rama
Japji: Meditation in Sikhism	Swami Rama
Lectures on Yoga	Swami Rama
Life Here and Hereafter	Swami Rama
Living with the Himalayan Masters	Swami Rama
Love and Family Life	Swami Rama
Love Whispers	Swami Rama
Meditation and Its Practice	Swami Rama
Nitnem	Swami Rama
Path of Fire and Light, Vol. I	Swami Rama
Path of Fire and Light, Vol. II	Swami Rama
Perennial Psychology of the Bhagavad Gita	Swami Rama
A Practical Guide to Holistic Health	Swami Rama
Sukhamani Sahib: Fountain of Eternal Joy	Swami Rama
The Valmiki Ramayana Retold in Verse	Swami Rama
The Wisdom of the Ancient Sages	Swami Rama
Creative Use of Emotion	Swami Rama, Swami Ajaya, Ph.D.
Science of Breath	Swami Rama, Rudolph Ballentine, M.D., Alan Hymes, M.D.
Yoga and Psychotherapy	Swami Rama, Rudolph Ballentine, M.D., Swami Ajaya, Ph.D.
The Mystical Poems of Kabir	Swami Rama, Robert Regli
Yoga-sutras of Patanjali	Usharbudh Arya, D.Litt.
Superconscious Meditation	Usharbudh Arya, D.Litt.
Mantra and Meditation	Usharbudh Arya, D.Litt.
Philosophy of Hatha Yoga	Usharbudh Arya, D.Litt.
Meditation and the Art of Dying	Usharbudh Arya, D.Litt.
God	Usharbudh Arya, D.Litt.
Psychotherapy East and West	Swami Ajaya, Ph.D.
Yoga Psychology	Swami Ajaya, Ph.D.

Diet and Nutrition	Rudolph Ballentine, M.D.
Joints and Glands Exercises	Rudolph Ballentine, M.D. (ed.)
Transition to Vegetarianism	Rudolph Ballentine, M.D.
Theory and Practice of Meditation	Rudolph Ballentine, M.D. (ed.)
Freedom from Stress	Phil Nuernberger, Ph.D.
Homeopathic Remedies	Dale Buegel, M.D., Blair Lewis, P.A.-C, Dennis Chernin, M.D., M.P.H.
Hatha Yoga Manual I	Samskrti and Veda
Hatha Yoga Manual II	Samskrti and Judith Franks
Seven Systems of Indian Philosophy	Rajmani Tigunait, Ph.D.
Shakti Sadhana: Steps to Samadhi	Rajmani Tigunait, Ph.D.
The Tradition of the Himalayan Masters	Rajmani Tigunait, Ph.D.
Yoga on War and Peace	Rajmani Tigunait, Ph.D.
Swami	Doug Boyd
Sikh Gurus	K.S. Duggal
Philosophy and Faith of Sikhism	K.S. Duggal
The Quiet Mind	John Harvey, Ph.D. (ed.)
Himalayan Mountain Cookery	Martha Ballentine
The Man Who Never Died	Dr. Gopal Singh
Yogasana for Health	Yogiraj Behramji
Meditation in Christianity	Himalayan Institute
Spiritual Journal	Himalayan Institute
Blank Books	Himalayan Institute

To order or to request a free mail order catalog call or write

The Himalayan Publishers
RR 1, Box 405
Honesdale, PA 18431
Toll-free 1-800-822-4547